Able
&
Equal

A Gentle Path to Peace

Denton L. Roberts

with Frances Thronson

Third Edition

Foreword by Michael Gavin

Not So Common Publishing

Publishing Services: AuthorImprints.com

Published by Not So Common Publishing, Christchurch, Dorset, United Kingdom

http://www.notsocommon.pub

Contents

Foreword

If I am not for myself, who is for me?
If I am for myself alone, what am I worth?
If not now, when?

Rabbi Hillel

Why now
Christchurch, Dorset, UK.
Early morning November 9th, 2016.

Having grown accustomed to a world with many unresolved conflicts, having watched the aftermath of the UK referendum on EU membership, the lead up to the US presidential election, and now its outcome, I thought: "If ever a Gentle Path to Peace was needed, it is now."

In a time when people seem to be feeling unacknowledged, undervalued and powerless to shape their circumstances, when there is division, recrimination, and a weakening of mutual esteem and fellow feeling, I wanted a way to make a positive contribution. A long-held notion—to see Able & Equal back in circulation—became a decision and a commitment. I wanted people to have an accessible theory, a simple practice, and a foundation of self-support and mutual esteem through Roberts' Healthy Core beliefs, so that those who choose would be well-resourced as peacemakers for the challenges of healing the hurts and rifts in our communities.

I had no idea how to go about the task of republishing a book. I had to learn something about what it means, in Denton Roberts' terms, to be Capable. It was not about knowing the ins and outs of publishing, copyright or other technicalities. It was about taking the first step, and then the next, and then the next. By diligence and good luck, I found Frances Thronson, the book's surviving co-author, who generously gave her co-operation. I found David Wogahn of AuthorImprints as an invaluable source of professional support. You have the result of these efforts in your hands, or on your screen.

Why This Book

From the first time that I read *Able and Equal,* in the late 1980s, I was captivated. These are the things that appealed to me:

- anatomising the idea of OKness into the 5 Healthy Core Beliefs
- the key question "Am I on my side, or on my case?"
- Self-esteem as Human Esteem—relational and beyond cultural restrictions
- the emphasis on gentleness

- Those five powerful words: Capable, Powerful, Valuable, Lovable, and Equal
- the Workbook exercises—the offer of a daily practice
- a focus on body awareness—attending to one's sensations
- the Path to Peace and Peacemaking

OKNESS

Like many people in the early 80s I was quite taken with the book "I am OK, You're OK." In time I came to see its limitations, but I am grateful because it led me to read Eric Berne, and thence to study Transactional Analysis(TA).

The TA concept of OKness is a mixed blessing. At its most profound "I am OK, You're OK" can point to the I-Thou relationship, the presence in each of us of one and the same divine spark. *But "I'm okay, you're okay" is a very fetching idea and one that intrigues, but for most of us, is little more than naive, aphoristic and characteristic of pop psychology."* (See page 129.)

When Denton Roberts anatomises OKness into the related Five Healthy Core Beliefs, Capable, Powerful, Valuable, Lovable, Equal, he turns it into something substantial, meaningful, and usable.

"Am I on my side, or on my case?"

In the later years of my practice I focused on working with trauma, and with supervising trauma therapists. Self-care in the face of trauma became an important theme for me. I found

Denton Roberts' practice invaluable for practitioners subjected to other peoples' intense stressors as well as their own. Too often, helpers have learned to disregard their own internal distress, responding to its echo in those they help, and failing to find a peaceful state within no matter how hard they strive on behalf of others.

This pivotal question, which Roberts describes as "self-confrontation," is so easily overlooked, and yet, just by itself can bring about a transformation of perspective, and experience.

Self-esteem and Human Esteem

The quest for self-esteem can come to have a flavour of desperation, a need to fill a perceived emptiness. Roberts reframes Self-Esteem as Human Esteem, an acknowledgement of qualities that all humans—including ourselves—are born with, and do not need to strive for, but to recognise and appreciate in ourselves and everyone. Human Esteem does not need to put another down to build itself up. It is not bound by the norms of any social or cultural group, but arises from our common humanity.

Gentleness

The antidote to striving that Roberts recommends is gentleness. *"Gentleness, as I have experienced it, is sensitive acceptance of ourselves, not syrupy sweetness or condescension. With sensitive acceptance of ourselves, creative ways of dealing with situations eventually occur to us. Gentleness is the lubricant of learning."* (See page 46.)

Attending to sensations

As a body psychotherapist, and somatic trauma therapist, I am acutely aware of the importance of body awareness as a link to the profound wisdom of the body. Roberts' approach, akin to Eugene Gendlin's Focusing, gives this somatic wisdom a central role in the daily practice. "The truth is in the body."(See page 135.)

Five powerful words: Capable, Powerful, Valuable, Lovable, Equal

I have yet to discover how Denton Roberts came up with this set of qualities. I find them compelling.

A Set of Practical Exercises

Books are wonderful: they transmit wisdom and experience, they convey ideas that can light up our minds. For lasting growth and change, these ideas need to be put into regular practice. Only by practice does what we learn from books become "second nature." For this reason, I was delighted to see, and have frequently used, the Workbook components of *Able and Equal*. When a concept becomes a practice, we have created something enduring.

For this reason, in addition to publishing the book, I have also created a course to support readers as they work steadily through the daily practices. You can find it and other resources at www.able-and-equal.me.

The Path to Peace and Peacemaking

From what I have learnt about Denton Roberts, as a pastor, as a therapist, and as a person, he was committed to building relationships and communities where mutual respect and affection blossomed. Taking the growth of personal esteem beyond the merely personal, and into the realm of social action, conflict resolution—both without and within—raises the quest for self-esteem and autonomy to another level. It addresses issues that have become manifestly urgent in our times.

In these troubled and troubling times, I believe this book meets a need to help people sustain themselves in the face of stress and conflict, and to sustain one another, and ultimately to bring mutual respect, mutual esteem, and healing to our divided communities.

This book attempts to make evident the foundation of okayness in an effort to demonstrate the necessity of human esteem. I'm okay, you're okay is an idea that points to a truth beyond itself; I believe Human Esteem serves the same purpose. (See page 130.)

Why me

In the twenty years, 1970 to 1990, that I worked in Special Education in some tough areas in Inner London—Stepney, Bermondsey, Camberwell and Peckham—with troubled and troublesome children and adolescents, as a teacher, Deputy Head, and Headteacher, I came to learn a lot about confrontation, challenge, about authority, compassion, desperation and resolution. Faced with young people who were hurt and angry, who had lost trust—often for good reason, who felt that their self-worth, indeed their survival, depended on aggression, it was not always easy to maintain an "I'm OK, you're OK" attitude. On the other hand, nothing else works.

When, towards the end of this time, I first read *Able and Equal*, it was a revelation. Nothing in my own life had prepared me for these challenges. What I learned, I learned the hard way, through many trials and many errors. Denton Roberts' ideas validated some of the things that I had learned for myself, and clarified others that had not been clear to me. It gradually dawned on me that I had in some sense learned to be a Peacemaker.

In my later career, as an education consultant on behaviour management, and then as a body psychotherapist, somatic trauma therapist, as a supervisor and trainer, the philosophy of *Able and Equal* was a cornerstone of my own practice and of what I offered to those I served.

In this present phase of my life, where the challenge is, according to Erik Erikson, to achieve Integrity in the face of Despair and Disgust, cited by Denton on page 110, I want to pass on what has been of such great value to me to those who, whatever their role and whether they know it are not, are called to Make Peace in our unsettled and seemingly divided world.

That is why I have found out how to get a book published. (Now I know, it may not be the last.) And that is why I have created the website www.able-and-equal.me where you can find other resources including the on-line course that will take you step by step through the daily Workbook practices. This material is too good not to put into practice, whichever way you choose to do it.

Michael Gavin

Publisher's Notes
on the Third Edition

If you are familiar with this book in its second (1987) edition, you will notice a couple of differences.

1. We have chosen not to include the paper "Structural Symbiotic Systems" by R.D.Phillips, MD. This is a fascinating monograph, by no means wholly irrelevant to the theme of *Able and Equal,* but rather more narrowly focused. The aim was to keep things simple, so the monograph has been excluded. We feared that, with its many tables and diagrams, the text would present technical problems in assembling the new version of the book. As it happens, these problems were minimal, so it has been possible to make a PDF version, which is available separately at www.able-and-equal.me.

2. For reasons I cannot fully explain, it has felt right to alter slightly the order in which the five *Core Healthy Beliefs* are presented, with Valuable coming third, and Lovable coming fourth in the list.

How to Use This Book

The heart of the book lies in the *Human Esteem Workbook Pages,* beginning on page 135.

If you are keen to get right down to work, begin with these. The instructions are clear and simple. If the practice gives rise to questions, scan the earlier chapters and follow Denton Roberts' thinking as it is laid out there.

Of course, you can do the normal thing: start at the beginning, and read through to the end. Be aware that if you decide not to do the practice, you are missing the part that can truly make a difference. Or you can wander through the book as your fancy takes you. When you land on the workbook pages, it will be best if you stop wandering, and focus for a while. However you read, enjoy.

If you find it difficult to persevere with the workbook pages, and would like a structured programme, go to www.able-and-equal.me where you will find resources to help you, including an online course that will take you step-by-step through the process, with daily emails and other resources.

Introduction

We're all searching for peace. This book provides a process through which we can actively develop the foundations of peace in our lives.

I see myself as a simplifier. I have identified five foundational core beliefs which we need before we can effectively pursue the establishment of peace on a personal, relational or international level and call these Healthy Core Beliefs. They are:

> I am a capable human being,
> I am a powerful human being,
> I am a valuable human being,
> I am a lovable human being
> and I and all humans are equal.

These Healthy Core Beliefs provide a foundation for psychological and spiritual well-being, just as nutrition and exercise provide a foundation for physiological well-being. When people function from the basis that they and all people are capable, powerful, valuable, lovable and equal, there exists what I identify as Human Esteem, which provides the bedrock upon which peace is built.

The primary concepts discussed in this book are stated briefly here:

1. Every human being is born a princess or prince. Early experiences have convinced some that they are frogs.
2. Individuals start off in an autonomous state.
3. Human Esteem is the recognition that healthy beliefs about ourselves are equally true for others.
4. The difference between whether we function autonomously or as victims is determined by what we believe about ourselves.
5. There are five Healthy Core Beliefs that provide the foundation of Human Esteem. They are: I and all people are capable, I and all people are powerful, I and all people are valuable, I and all people are lovable, and I and all people are equal.
6. Gentleness is a powerful human resource that is often neglected, particularly in self-treatment.
7. There are two primary ways that we relate and feel about ourselves and others: being *for* or being *against*. We *choose* how we relate.
8. Behavior patterns established in early experiences and reinforced throughout life can cause us to be "on our case" (against) when we need to be "on our side" (for).

9. Positive self-confrontation is the most effective way to stimulate change and using it intentionally strengthens our sense of autonomy.

10. Core beliefs are the foundation of the belief systems we use to direct our lives.

11. Fight, flight and resolution are options available when faced with problems/issues.

12. Energy is always moving—either toward creativity or defensiveness.

13. Affirming that we are adequate is the first and essential step in accomplishing our goals.

14. Whether we view self, others and world as okay is determined by our core beliefs.

Human Esteem

By presenting the idea of Human Esteem rather than Self-esteem I am seeking to avoid the limitations of the concept of self-esteem. Self-esteem is limited because it is culturally defined and the qualities individuals esteem in themselves will be determined by the qualities their cultures value. I define Human Esteem as the mutual valuing that occurs between people based on a comprehension of our *alikeness and relatedness*, regardless of culture, the historical era in which we live, our sex or race. It is interpersonal—something within and between persons, that, when present, will allow them to discover more and more of themselves and others. It is the same phenomenon that allows us to feel a sense of relationship with Beethoven, Buddha,

Stone Age cave painters and Mother Theresa, regardless of the time or distance between us. Esteem based on mutuality in no way lessens appreciation of differences, and is not a matter of reducing humanity, in all its varieties of raiment, to its lowest common denominator—in fact it encourages just the opposite. Whenever we recognize our own distinctive value regardless of culturally imposed criteria, we can be aware of that same—and different—distinctiveness and value in all others.

By encouraging thought about Human Esteem I hope to assist in identifying those qualities that help us know we are autonomous beings, determined not by the cultural norms of our society and time but ultimately by our deepest and truest selves. We are inextricably connected to all other beings, yet possess the power to define and shape our individual identities into a form that is both unique to us and complementary with the highest of humanity. As we grasp this interrelatedness we will be less bound to the daily problem-solving tasks of life and will be able to relate ourselves more completely to the establishment of peace and harmony in human relations.

The Problem of Autonomy

Eric Berne said of autonomy: "Parents, deliberately or unaware, teach their children from birth how to behave, think, feel and perceive. Liberation from these influences is no easy matter, since they are deeply ingrained and are necessary during the first two or three decades of life for biological and social survival. Indeed, such liberation is only possible at all because the individual starts off in an autonomous state, that is, capable of awareness, spontaneity and intimacy, and he has some discretion as to which parts of his parents' teachings he will accept."

Berne's awareness that individuals start off in an autonomous state has profound implications for both our concepts of self and others. From the small child, announcing with determination "Me do it, me do it," to the college student receiving a diploma, to the carpenter stepping back and surveying a completed job, we strive and search for, succeed and fail at the condition of being self-governing. Autonomy can be described as the power we possess, used or unused, to direct our energy to create our individual lives. The question of whether we will take advantage of it, claim it as our own, is the most persistent and recurring issue we face.

I once worked as a speech therapist with a twelve-year-old boy who was born with a double cleft palate, cleft lip, club foot and a deformed hand. His father was a rough-hewn man who ran a parts department in the local car dealership and his mother taught elementary school. His father told me of his response when he first saw his son with a gaping hole in his mouth, a turned-in foot, and missing fingers on one hand,—he said to himself, "this young man is going to get everything he needs." When I met him he talked with the familiar "honk" of most cleft palate children. I asked him what he wanted to be and he said in his nearly unintelligible voice "I'm going to be a surgeon like the surgeons who fixed me up." I had great difficulty understanding the word surgeon and had to ask him to repeat it two or three times. As we worked together, the ability to say surgeon so that people could understand it was our primary goal. This young man had many limitations but I was impressed with his ability to constantly approach life with great vitality. We worked for six weeks during that summer, primarily on sounds that he could not make before the summer began. Never did he become discouraged. Again and again he exercised the muscles necessary in order to make that "s" and "r" sound. By the time the summer ended, I felt inspired by this experience of knowing and working with a person who chose to focus on what he *could* do and how he *could* express himself. I wondered, with all of these handicaps, how he maintained such vitality. From birth he had been in and out of hospitals, operation after operation, correcting his physical limitations. He had been laughed at, teased and misunderstood on the playgrounds of the school and yet he had zeal for life and a sense of the direction for his life. He was being autonomous, not allowing the responses of others to entirely determine his identity. In the face of other kids making fun of him, parents' efforts to overprotect him or teachers who thought he couldn't learn, he remained as true as he could to his own true self.

My wife, who died two weeks before publication of the first edition of this book, spent the last seven-and-a-half years of her life facing a fatal disease. The first time we visited the specialist after we knew that the disease was fatal the specialist turned to me and asked "How is her attitude?" I said, "Jerry has always been long on attitude." After a thoughtful pause he said "Life is very short any way we look at it, and attitude is all we are truly in charge of." Autonomy can be viewed as the power to take charge of our own attitude.

By viewing autonomy as the power to guide and direct our lives, rather than be directed by circumstance, we maintain our vitality and are better able to negotiate whatever circumstances we encounter. If we fail to see autonomy as our own power to self-govern and see it instead as a condition dictated by fate, we drift toward viewing ourselves as victims each time the circumstances of life become difficult. To understand and to nourish our power to self-govern is essential. My young friend and my wife were both good examples of what happens when we claim autonomy as a power. When we're generally successful at getting what we want we are naturally aware of our autonomy and support it. During those times when we're less successful and things just don't seem to be going our way, we tend to be unaware of our autonomy and feel helpless and hopeless. The issue of how to move from the feelings of helplessness and despair we all experience to a sense of our power to govern and direct our lives is the central theme of this book.

A Note about the Second Edition

In this second edition we have answered some problems that were brought to our attention by readers of the first edition. In the first edition the idea of Healthy Core Beliefs was linked with the concept of peace on the simple theory that when the individual becomes peaceful, peace will also permeate all relationships, institutions and society. In this edition we have greatly expanded and elaborated the Healthy Core Belief material and have added a considerable number of new concepts to the text as a whole. The peacemaking section has been placed after the main body of the text in order that the reader will more fully comprehend the relatedness of Healthy Core Beliefs and peacemaking. Adam Curle, a leading Quaker peacemaker and former Professor of Peace Studies at Harvard University spoke to the condition of relatedness between personal and public peace aptly when he said:

> "Peacemaking is the science of perceiving
> that things that appear to be apart are one.
> It is the art of restoring love to a relationship
> from which it has been driven by fear and hatred....
> Public peacemaking is what we do;
> private peacemaking is what we are,
> the two are interpenetrating."

The Beginning

"Every human being is born a prince or a princess; early experiences convince some that they are frogs..." When I first read this simple idea presented by Eric Berne, I experienced a revolution in my thought. The way I viewed myself and others altered dramatically as I considered the possibility that this idea was true. It was easy to recognize that every infant I'd ever seen was a princess or a prince; it was a bit more difficult to recognize that *every* individual I'd ever encountered was a princess or a prince, but I could, with effort. My most difficult task was to recognize this truth about myself. As I gave these ideas serious attention and thought, I changed my self-concept. Since first encountering Berne's thought, I've looked for other basic truths that provide enhanced Human Esteem and have questioned the assumption that the route to healthy psychological functioning is necessarily complex. Could there be a few simple truths that, when well-established in the psyche, provide a foundation for Human Esteem? Could it be that *we can and do* establish such truths regularly and systematically throughout life by our own thoughts?

Having gained a new sense of freedom and value from the idea that every human being is born a princess or a prince, I began searching for the basic truths we need established in our psyches in order to support personal peace and fulfillment. Human Esteem, I am proposing, is a way of believing and behaving toward self and others that provides a framework through which *human commonality* is the basis for interaction rather than societally established and defined standards. George Leonard, in his book *The Silent Pulse*, comments "...it is possible to conceive of each human individual as *consisting* of pure information expressed as rhythmic waves that start as the infinitesimal vibrations of subatomic particles and build outward as ever-widening resonant hierarchies of atoms, molecules, cells, organs, organisms, families, bands, tribes, nations, civilizations, and beyond. At every step along the way, every entity is connected to the great web of information that is the universe. At the most fundamental level, the connection is not sensory but structural, for we are not *in* but *of* the web of relationship. As part of the web, each of us *is* an individual identity, and that identity can be most easily expressed as a wave function, a unique rhythmic pulse.... Thus, we are both individual and universal, and the web of relationship involves both aspects of our being. Though all the information of the universe is ultimately available in each of us, the amount of it we can encode and express—a tiny amount, indeed—is limited by our particular history, culture, language, and nervous system." Self-esteem, as opposed to Human Esteem, is built upon a concept of self in accord with the norms of a given society. Human esteem differs from Self-esteem at a values level. Self-esteem is established on socially reinforced values and Human Esteem is based on values that are true for all of humanity. Human Esteem avoids the prejudices and biases of a given society. Today, as never before in history, it is critically important for us to discover the basic truths that unite all humanity if we are going to survive. Human Esteem provides a view of ourselves in relationship to all humanity: a wholeness that reinforces both our individual autonomy and our corporate relatedness, providing a basis upon which we can discover how to live harmoniously.

The need for Human Esteem is reflected in the wisdom of the first sentence of the Declaration of Independence. The founders of the United States were aware that in order for them to function autonomously, they needed to do two things: first, support themselves and secondly, hold a decent respect for the opinions of humankind. They realized and clearly articulated that what is valuable for themselves must of necessity also be valuable for all humanity: "When in the course of human events it becomes necessary for one people to dissolve the political bonds which connects them to another, and to assume among the powers of the earth the separate and equal stations to which the laws of nature and of nature's God have entitled them, a decent respect of the opinions of mankind require that they declare the causes which impelled them to the separation."

Human Esteem embraces both individual autonomy and a decent respect for the opinions and autonomy of others. Human

Esteem, unlike self-esteem, exists as an interpersonal phenomenon and exists when individuals recognize that that which is valid for them is equally valid for all.

Having gained a new perspective from personally grappling with the idea that each one of us is inherently valuable, I realized that when my concept of self is built on a false premise, it results in a distorted view of both myself and others; I began to wonder if there are a few pivotal ideas we each need to have in focus in order to claim our autonomy and value others at the same time. Further, could it be that the many complex and confounding problems we all encounter are intrinsically connected to issues of human esteem? Since that time I've searched for the beliefs that, when established in our psyches, support autonomy. Human Esteem is built on beliefs that encourage creative resolution of the whole spectrum of life problems—from personal to international.

Like it or not, life energy is all we've got to spend. How we spend our energy is determined by our attitudes and decisions. In the final analysis, we spend energy either creatively or defensively. If we spend it creatively life is vital; if we spend our energy defensively, life is a burden and a chore. What makes the difference between whether we deal creatively with issues or whether we deal defensively with issues is a pressing question. By being aware that every event is an exchange of energy we can move to take charge of how we spend our energy.

While working on a new church and community center recently, I realized that every piece put in place involved an exchange of energy. The tree grew with the energy of the planet; the wood was milled with harnessed energy, purchased through the energy of the contributors, it was lifted off the truck, measured, cut to fit and nailed down with the workers' energy. It occurred to me that everything that happened in that building, for good or ill, would occur through an exchange of energy. As we recognize that all we have to spend in life is energy we, become very purposeful about how we spend it. Some elect to use their energy to deal with "what is" creatively, while others are devastated, if not destroyed, by the "what is" of their lives. I suspect that this elusive difference is intimately related to esteem of self and others—Human Esteem.

James Masterson, in his studies of the borderline personality, has divided the issues addressed in therapy into three broad categories: fate, nature, and nurture.

Fate issues are characterized by those things determined by events over which we truly have no control, such as the governing political system of the country in which we are born, and the circumstances of our families.

Nature issues are those determined by genetic structure—physical limitations, strengths, ethnicity, the way we look.

Nurture issues relate to the amount of caring and support that we receive from our early environments. Masterson terms this "maternal libidinal availability," which, simply stated, could be called availability of caring energy.

By dividing these life issues into three categories we can determine where to most productively spend our energy. Energy spent on fate and nature issues is only productive when used to understand the implications and impositions these facts have on our lives. For example, it is important to understand the implications—both positive and negative—of growing up with a physically ill parent, but it is counterproductive to use such an historical fact to feel deprived or exceptional throughout our life. Likewise, it is important to *accept* our physical being and *counterproductive* to constantly wish we had blue eyes instead of brown. Granted, many issues are not so clear cut and contain a mixture of fate, nature and nurture considerations. The sorting out of these issues provides us with very real benefits and is worth significant amounts of our consideration and energy. Once we've sorted through these issues we will have a much clearer perspective on ourselves and the issues that need to simply be understood and accepted and the issues that we can address effectively. This clarity and knowing where to focus deepens our sense of personal autonomy.

Nurture issues relate to using time and attention in such a way that our needs and the needs of others are provided for. Sometimes this can be pleasant and immediately gratifying and other times it is just plain hard work. Spending our energy arranging for nourishing environments that allow growth is utilizing our autonomy productively. To the extent that we experience ourselves as capable of taking care of the business of our lives and arranging our environments to include those things that we enjoy, we will feel autonomous. And to the extent we feel incapable of arranging our environments so that they are nourishing, our days become a drudge and we experience ourselves as *victims*. We have all developed habits of taking care of ourselves that relate directly to our childhood experiences and these habits determine the extent to which we think of ourselves as *autonomous* or as *victims*. By thinking through our basic beliefs and applying our insights to issues of esteem, we can conclude that the expression of our autonomy resides in two places: first, the ability to understand and assimilate our fate and nature issues, and second, our ability to develop for ourselves nurturing structures that give us reliable sources of caring. To the extent we have reliable sources of caring available, our esteem of self and others flow naturally.

The Path of
Healthy Core Beliefs

My intention has been to find the Healthy Core Beliefs people
need to experience themselves as *autonomous individuals*,
able to cope creatively with anything from everyday criticism
to the possibility of nuclear holocaust. I believe that autonomous persons live with others recognizing and respecting one
another's autonomy and creating a cooperative environment.
In an effort to help others devise means of strengthening autonomy, I've utilized my background in the fields of psychology and
grass-roots social service institutions, as well as observing my
own personal process. Repeatedly, I've found that by strengthening Healthy Core Beliefs, people are freed of undue dependence
on external circumstances and events for their sense of value and
autonomy; instead, value and autonomy are internally stimu-
lated and sustained. Whenever a person's self-concept is built
on a foundation that adequately supports Human Esteem, that
person is able to withstand tremendous stress and strain and still
live creatively—without the spirit being destroyed. Conversely,

when one's self-concept does not have a healthy foundation even the slightest circumstantial stress can be devastating.

As I wrote the first edition of this book, my wife of 25 years was in the final days of a terminal illness. During the seven years of living with imminent death, we had to squarely face one of life's most powerful confrontations. Early on we realized that our only choices were in the attitudes we took to the circumstances we were in. We could be morose, hostile, devastated, sad, etc. We had to choose how to spend life's quickly dwindling moments. We had to deliberately and intentionally take charge of our attitudes toward our circumstances.

A truth, when finally discovered, often turns out to be simple. Einstein said that understanding relativity meant that one was able to explain it to a twelve-year-old. In my search for the truths that undergird Human Esteem, I've looked for those simple truths that are self-evident in daily life and have sought to organize my findings so that persons can relate to them from their own experience.

Simple truths are like time bombs in the psyche. Once they explode open, they affect the arrangement of our whole life. As I mentioned before, when I first read Berne's words "Every human being is born a prince or princess" they radically changed the way I perceived life around me and my actions in that system. Prior to this time, some of my interactions with others were based on my being a victim of semi-tragic circumstances of fate and nature which I began to recognize as manipulative, though that manipulation was most often out of my awareness.

My major "fate" issue was that my father was killed in an accident before I was born, and my "nature" issue was a genetic predisposition to handle stress through gastro-intestinal disorders (I had perforated an ulcer by the time I was nineteen). I used these facts to "prove" I was a victim and that became what Berne called a "racket"—an unconscious way to emotionally extort recognition and nurture from others. I could see that I'd used both these fate and nature issues to gain considerable attention and maintain my image of myself and the "facts of my life." I found the idea of giving up this world view and the notion that I was indeed a prince, paradoxically confronting and liberating—hard to swallow and extremely appealing. I'd used fate and nature issues all my life to gain attention and nurturing, but knew that this attention and care was for the "poor little boy" part of me and not the real me, the whole, capable and creative person I knew myself to be. Because the recognition was for this "victim" part, I discounted it too, not even truly letting in the caring and attention I did receive. The simple truth that I was born a prince began a profound rearrangement of the way I perceived myself and others. Once I changed my belief about myself, I began to arrange for attention and nurture in more fulfilling ways; I also found my work as a psychotherapist becoming increasingly effective because I could not be easily hooked into my clients' "victim" mentality.

The Desire to Change

When we want change, it's natural to search for new ideas, insights and knowledge that will give us a new perspective help us effect the changes we want. We're always looking for something to make a "light" go on and provide illumination. Paradoxically, we resist new ideas and insights because once we uncover them it can be frightening and/or threatening to change. Many of our most firmly held beliefs about life were developed in order to feel safe during difficult and painful experiences when we were very young. We have grown to take these beliefs for granted and, generally out of our awareness, hold dim memories of ways in which they once comforted us. We think these beliefs provide safety and, perhaps more important, almost infallible methods and formulas to follow in dealing with the people and events of life. To acknowledge that these "tried and true" recipes of old we've relied on may be more of a hindrance than a help can leave us feeling very vulnerable and uncertain. Beliefs about ourselves and the world provide a structure through which we assimilate experiences and this structure is linked together, much like a bridge, providing us a means of safe transport. Intuitively we recognize that once we start taking pieces of the bridge apart, and before we've replaced those parts with new, more structurally sound pieces, we are placing ourselves in jeopardy. It is this intuitive wisdom that incorporating new beliefs and abandoning old beliefs will call *all* of our beliefs into question which is frightening. It will necessitate change and may cause internal conflict.

Not too long ago a client came into a session very tense and agitated—he anxiously paced the office and told me he was on the verge of a nervous breakdown. This man was seriously concerned about his mental health and felt desperate about his situation. I was chewing tobacco at the time and had put a fresh chew into my mouth just before he came in. (For those of you who aren't familiar with the process, soon after a fresh chew goes in, a whole lot of excess saliva wants to come out.) As his story progressed, my need to use the spittoon beside the desk demanded more and more of my attention. When he finally paused to catch his breath, I took the opportunity to use my spittoon. Caught unawares by this startlingly inappropriate response to the gravity of his situation, he laughed abruptly and said, "Damn you, Denton, I didn't think I'd ever laugh again!" For that one moment the conviction that his situation was hopeless flew right out from under him and his attention shifted from obsession with his own internal state to the events of the immediate present. He responded spontaneously, unburdened momentarily by his belief that all was lost; by allowing a percentage of his focus to move away from his belief that he was trapped in tragic circumstances to simply observing events in the present, his emotional state changed. His acknowledged resistance to laughter was a clue that he wanted, at some level, to maintain the belief that he was a victim.

Another example of this shift is the common experience of feeling melancholic, lonely, perhaps even despairing, and then getting a phone call from a good friend. After the call, our perspective on life is different. What happened is that a shift in our thinking has occurred; we've been reminded of friendship and have heard about the dilemmas and progress of our friend's life. When our *thoughts* change we experience changes in our feelings.

These illustrations indicate that we are always, to some extent, resistant to the notion of changing our perspective. By not changing our perspective we consciously and unconsciously keep our environment familiar. No one likes to be proven wrong and we assume a position that we believe to be right. Our unique position, or posture, develops constantly throughout life and provides a sense of security, enables procurement of our basic needs, enhances our individual identity and facilitates contact with other beings. Throughout our developmental process, each piece of the structure is built by our experiences and consists of our very best thinking at that time. Once adopted this position is reinforced both negatively and positively and becomes basic to our security. Such a highly developed, hard fought and thoroughly tested existential position is then protected through that which can be identified as resistances and defense mechanisms.

To illustrate this propensity, in ancient Judaism, whenever a concept was accepted as the word of God it became Law. Those who were charged with keeping the Law built rules to insure against accidental violations of the Law. This process was called "building a fence around the Torah." This protection process of that which is sacred in religion and society is paralleled in the human organism by protecting, with resistances and defenses, those hard-fought, experientially discovered truths which are the building blocks of our basic position.

Many of us feel an illogical resistance to the concept of equality between the sexes. These resistances are founded on a well reinforced belief in male supremacy. As these beliefs begin to be challenged and I hope, abandoned, the roles of men and women change and traditional lines of authority are redefined. In making this change the equilibrium of both the society and the family are temporarily rearranged. The price of clinging to beliefs in male supremacy is great when we realize that to hold to it we must exclude from awareness many injustices, not the least of which is ignoring the historic and current accomplishments of women. Changing such a fundamental belief system which affects authority, structure and tradition is a herculean task. It calls on us to establish societal and family patterns that preserve the positive values of the past and at the same time develop a system that does not impose arbitrary limitations based on biology or traditional family roles. Currently, the few who have overcome their resistances are watching with excitement as their daughters develop greater opportunities for self-determination.

As new roles within the family emerge, we will witness the next generation growing up with a sense of autonomy based on equality. By overcoming current resistances and reconstructing our belief system to include equality between the sexes, we stimulate a new vitality in the relationships between men and women and a new vitality in society as a whole.

Similarly, many of us were raised with the belief that those over a certain age and those under a certain age had very little to contribute. As long as we hold that belief, we exclude or discount the value of the wisdom of the old and the vitality of the young. By changing that belief we open doors to the resources that the young and old offer us all.

These large-scale "remodeling" jobs on our belief systems have never proven to be smooth, easy or painless tasks because they "go against the grain" of popular society as well as our own internal programming. Those who do challenge ingrained and detrimental beliefs stand to gain a new respect for the strength and viability of their own autonomy and a heightened awareness and sensitivity to the impact of *all* beliefs on the lives of other people.

Although we constantly search for new truths and insights, we also frequently resist them. Resistances range from "I know that so I don't have to think about it" to "I wish I had known that 20 years ago but it's too late now." Resistances are healthy because they prevent us from taking in information that would radically disturb our equilibrium—information that we are not prepared to assimilate. Resistances can also be detrimental because they encourage automatic disregard of valuable information.

Recent studies show that mental health and maturity are based on an individual's ability to recognize and reconcile that there is both good and bad in all people, themselves included. To be raised with the belief that people are either good or bad, is a great detriment to mental health and maturity. When we expand our belief system to recognize that there is good and bad in all people and that there are no totally good or totally bad people in the world, our ability to accept and understand ourselves and our ability to accept and understand others is vastly enlarged.

We are unlikely to unquestioningly accept any new idea we encounter; the ideas, or "truths" that we ultimately accept are those which resonate with our intuition and experience. The truths based on both intuition and experience become beliefs. When we see a cube, we never see all sides of it at once. Yet we "know" it as a cube and we "know" a cube has six sides. It could have no bottom and no far wall, and still appear to be a cube. I know it to be a figure of three sides and I *believe* it to be a figure of six sides based on intuition, instinct and experience. We know ourselves through what we've been taught and what we've experienced. This knowledge needs to be linked with the intuitive/instinctual truth we all 'know' about ourselves. When this occurs we form Healthy Core Beliefs. Foundational beliefs are based on learning and experience that is congruent with our intuitive knowledge about ourselves and others.

This book is about the five Healthy Core Beliefs human beings need to support their growth, development and the pursuit of happiness. These Healthy Core Beliefs are that each one of us is capable, powerful, valuable, lovable, and equal. Most of us will attest to these beliefs in theory, but would probably debate whether some or all humans manifest these qualities. To manifest these qualities individually and in relationships, individuals first need to learn how to support Healthy Core Beliefs about themselves. Holding a core belief that is congruent with intuitive/instinctual information provides a healthy foundation from which to assimilate life experience. As we form relationships based on core beliefs that *we and others* are capable, powerful, valuable, lovable and equal, we are able to solve problems as they occur. Persons functioning with Healthy Core Beliefs create an interpersonal field that allows for creativity. Hugh Prather, author and psychologist, describes this phenomenon and its product as follows:

"After dinner Oliver came over and sat next to Mr. Mayer, who was across the room from me on the couch. They introduced themselves, then I watched that miracle that sometimes happens when two people come together and at once their minds synchronize. That has happened to me, and there are times when I feel myself striving to bring it about again, especially if I am talking to someone I have just met. When it comes unforced, the phenomenon is almost supernatural. As in some moments of love, there is a feeling of each of us being totally contained within the other. I begin surprising myself with what I say. I state insights that an instant before I didn't know I was capable of. Were they always inside me, but now this person is pulling them out? It feels more nearly as if together we have formed a new mind which until that moment did not exist."

The "new mind" Prather identifies is the consciousness I call Human Esteem and is the basis of intimacy, peace and autonomy. The five core beliefs that form the foundation of Human Esteem are: 1. I am a capable human; 2. I am a powerful human; 3.I am a valuable human; 4. I am a lovable human; 5. I and *all humans* are equal. These core beliefs, when they are well-established in our self-concept, provide us with internal psychological support and allow us to see our fellow humans as capable, powerful, valuable, lovable and equal.

It is when we see ourselves and others as capable, powerful, valuable, lovable, and equal, that we develop what I call Human Esteem. Human Esteem, as defined before, is an interpersonal phenomenon—something within and between persons—that when present, will allow people to discover more and more *of themselves and others*. Anyone inclined to pick up a book titled *Able and Equal* is a person who is motivated to discover more about herself or himself, as well as others. I invite you to consider these Healthy Core Beliefs as the foundation upon which you can consciously strengthen your sense of autonomy, and live in a nurturing and nourishing relationship with self and others. As you contemplate these core beliefs, normal healthy resistances may come into play. Consider and think through what these resistances are based upon and where they came from. As you examine your resistances, you will become aware of some of the origins of your current beliefs. If you discover that these beliefs are incongruent with what you now know, you will begin a process of modifying your belief systems. By contemplating the Healthy Core Beliefs you will deepen your understanding of the premises on which you currently operate and be better able to see their effect on the shape and direction of your life. I have found that thinking through beliefs is in itself liberating, and adopting one's own Healthy Core Beliefs (not necessarily mine) is what allows persons to conclude that they are *able and equal*.

Let us turn our attention now to the five healthy core beliefs that are the foundations of Human Esteem. As you contemplate these core beliefs, remember to evaluate any resistances you might have and use them to provoke thought.

The
Five Healthy Core Beliefs

Capable

We're forever being confronted with tasks; some of them as routine as brushing our teeth, some as extraordinary as assimilating the loss of a loved one. The core belief that tells us we are capable human beings provides the foundation necessary for us to take up the routine and extraordinary tasks life presents. I have found that life doesn't offer fully developed adults tasks they are not capable of handling. Nonetheless, we regularly encounter tasks which we do not believe ourselves capable of handling. In these situations we must first strengthen our belief that we are capable. As with all the core beliefs, it's important to focus conscious thought on the belief that we are capable in order to stay psychologically fit.

Here are some thoughts about capable that can be found in the Workbook section:

Capable means I have the skills necessary to pursue my wants and realize many of my ambitions.

Capable means I have the ability to contribute to the well-being of myself and others.

Capable means I have the ability to cope with what life is, right here and now, however difficult.

Capable means I have the ability to develop and sustain nourishing and stimulating contact with others.

Capable means that I and others can peacefully resolve problems.

Powerful

Powerful means we influence our environment. Power is not bad in and of itself, but too frequently we associate power with negative and exploitative actions. By believing we are powerful, we acknowledge that our thoughts and actions influence those around us. There is no question that we are powerful. The questions lie in how we choose to use our power. A depressed person, whether he or she chooses to be aware of it, has a profound impact on others. Even self-deprecating people wield great power. Their constant self-put-downs are uncomfortable and irritating to listen to; they are thinly disguised manipulations for reassurance which, when given, fall on deaf ears. This represents a powerful move to maintain the center of attention at all times. By recognizing that we are powerful in every action, we can consciously choose the ways in which we use power.

Once we acknowledge and support our power, our need to demonstrate that power in self- or other-destructive ways will dissolve and we are more likely to use power in ways that are equitable rather than exploitative. Power is an issue that often comes into prominence in work settings. An employer who is aware of being personally powerful is more likely to use authority in a sensitive and humane fashion than someone in the same position who is uncertain of his or her power. The task of parenting, when one possesses a sense of power, is not threatening or overwhelming—it's still not an easy job, but with security in self, whatever tasks are faced seem "do-able." When two people are maintaining a relationship and each is aware of personal power, change can be negotiated without undue conflict, personal animosity or hurt, while if they do not believe themselves to be powerful, change is likely to be threatening, conflictive and bitter.

Once we acknowledge and support our power, our sense of autonomy expands and we curtail exploitative uses of power.

Here are some thoughts about powerful from the Workbook:

Powerful means that I recognize and acknowledge my influence and choose how I will use it.

Powerful means that every bite of food I eat becomes energy I utilize to express myself in the world.

Powerful means that others respond to me by the way I present myself.

Powerful means that I shape today along with the 5 billion others who share this period of history.

Powerful means that I have as much influence on those around me as they have on me.

Valuable

We are valuable simply by virtue of the fact that we exist. Our conscious and unconscious efforts to survive make *implicit* statements about our own inherent sense of value. In even the most primitive forms of life there is a built-in desire to survive, self-actualize and fulfill purpose. *Explicit* evidence of our value is socially reinforced through family, friends and achievement. Because this *explicit* evidence is left in the hands of others, that is, culturally defined and reinforced, we are not encouraged to remember that we are also valuable *simply because we exist*. A child that is repeatedly told to "be good" receives an explicit message that he or she is not naturally "good." This child will probably grow up feeling that his or her natural responses are not good enough. All too often awareness of our value comes primarily from the recognition we receive from others; often that recognition is contingent upon behavior that will be "approved" of and may well be in conflict with our internal sense of direction and self—we may be fulfilling others instead of ourselves. When we begin to *explicitly* reinforce the core belief that we are innately valuable, we take the matter into our own hands rather than leaving it to others, society and fate; our true self will emerge when primary reinforcement of our value comes from within. We develop a "false self" when we put the determination of our value in the hands of others. The smiles and frowns of those around us are seen as more important than our own expression, satisfaction and fulfillment but we are generally unaware that this is the case. Pleasing others is ingrained in us so thoroughly that we remain blind to what the spontaneous expression of our "true self" might be. When we know that we are valuable we escape the limits imposed by pleasing others and support our natural expression of that true self.

These expressions of the "true self" value human life above all else, therefore an acid test of whether or not we are acting on behalf of the true self is to ask whether *achieving our goals will benefit humanity as a whole*. Human beings will go to extreme lengths to get affirmation that they are valuable, as is characterized by clothes, cars, condos and careers. When we recognize that we *are* valuable by virtue of our existence, our *values* are likely to change and we are much less likely to be manipulated by the promises of contemporary culture. Whether we are speaking about the promises of Brooke Shields in her Calvins or The American Way, Love It or Leave It, contemporary culture always promises to provide happiness for those who are willing to adopt and strive for its values. By relying on the values espoused by any particular segment of contemporary culture rather than discovering the values of our own core self, our world-view becomes limited and cut off from human *commonality*. It is based instead on an *us against them* mentality. Immediately the question of whether our goals will benefit humanity as a whole becomes irrelevant, because humanity as a whole itself is irrelevant and in many ways, unnoticed. Rather than discovering and valuing the stirrings of our own inner self, adhering to external value systems keeps us constantly striving to meet the criteria of outer value systems—whether "yuppiedom" or political supremacy for the U.S. In fact, no one can actually meet all the criteria of externally imposed value systems, nor can any such system ultimately provide peace of mind. Our values can be seen as the outward and physical manifestation of our inward and spiritual condition. A first step toward freedom from the merry-go-round of externally dictated value systems and the inherently unsatisfying and empty nature of caring only for self is to thoughtfully consider just what values we desire for our inward spiritual condition. Values are to valuable as water is to thirst—water quenches thirst and values nourish, affirm the value of our truest nature.

Ironically, many resist the idea that they are innately valuable because that idea threatens to displace the enculturated symbols they have attained to prove that they are valuable. Many of our values symbolized by clothes, cars, condos and careers, pale in the face of values implied by Human Esteem. Consequently, until we are ready for a reorientation of the symbols of personal success, we will resist the belief that we and all people are valuable.

What is it about believing we are innately valuable (or capable, powerful, lovable, equal) that creates an internal environment supportive of the natural expression of our true self rather than our "pleasing self"? In the act of *believing*, we link volition, our conscious, intentional thought, with the built-in yearning to fulfill and self-actualize—by combining conscious thought and unconscious desire, we establish a serviceable mechanism, a powerful tool, for growth and wholeness.

Here are some thoughts about valuable from the Workbook:

Valuable means that I have worth because I exist.

Valuable means I have something to offer.

Valuable means I can enjoy.

Valuable means I accept my importance.

Valuable means there is sense to every aspect of my experience.

Lovable

We know we are lovable when are free to give and receive positive attention. To the extent that I believe I am lovable, I arrange my life to have people around me with whom I can exchange positive energy. Positive energy exchanges feel good and negative energy exchanges feel bad—both provide needed stimulation and recognition.

Believing that we are lovable has two dimensions: one, the giving of love, and two, the receiving of love. Both dimensions need to be open for us to lead a balanced life. When both are open, we are free to exchange caring. To the extent that we are aware of ourselves as lovable, we maintain a perspective that encourages us to feel we have choices and options in how we relate to others in our daily routine and are much less likely to see in others' words and actions rejection or criticism. Ultimately our perspective conditions everything from whether we feel good or bad about the weather. To the extent that we fail to recognize we are lovable, our perspective is likely to be dominated by feeling needy, even desperate for affection, attention and appreciation and we are likely to interpret others' words, deeds and thoughts as critical and "on our case." In *Scripts People Live*, Claude Steiner notes rather simply that positive strokes (units of recognition) feel good and negative strokes (units of recognition) feel bad. To the extent that I'm unwilling to believe I'm lovable, I am likely to interpret, attract and even unconsciously encourage recognition that will feel bad; to the extent that I believe I am lovable, I consciously and unconsciously attract attention that feels good.

Here are some thoughts about lovable from the Workbook:

Lovable means I can relate to myself and others in a warm and nourishing way.

Lovable means that each feeling I have is unique.

Lovable means that I feel I am individual and precious to myself and others.

Lovable means that I grow and have a sense of well-being when I give and receive nurturing.

Lovable means that I can create environments in which the human spirit will flourish.

Equal

The concept that we are equal is an ideal held by many and truly believed by few. Throughout our lives we're constantly bombarded by ideas, actions and insinuations that contradict this ideal. In order to comprehend equality, it is necessary to think in terms of *being* and not *doing*. Undeniably, people have differing abilities when it comes to *doing* and these abilities are based on everything from genetics to available opportunities. To obscure the issue even further, there exist seemingly universal societal prejudices. Good examples are that men are more valuable than women and that the rich deserve more veneration than the less well-off. While these are prejudices that have nothing to do with human worth or equality, to the extent that we're influenced by these ideas, we will view ourselves as superior or inferior—in other words, worth more or less than others. Usually we "major" in one and "minor" in the other, which is to say that we don't hold exclusively to a superior or inferior position, but rather vacillate between them. As long as we're influenced by ideas of superiority and inferiority, we will neither experience ourselves as equal nor will we recognize the equality of others.

A physician/psychiatrist who attended a workshop I was conducting argued the idea of equality at length until he finally realized that as long he viewed people exclusively through culturally supported values and hereditary talents, all of which had to do with *doing*, he would continue to vacillate between positions of superiority and inferiority in behavior and in relation to others. He concluded that "Equality is a *being* and not a *doing* issue." Insofar as we support our own equality and the ideal that "all people are equal" we are in a position to understand and relate to one another on a basis of *sameness* rather than *difference*. Focusing on similarities of desires, feelings and actions encourages the creation of a tie uniting us in the commonality and oneness that corresponds with humankind's highest ideals.

The infant comes into life with an innate sense of equality (being) that is not based on its capacities (doing). By nature it uses every one of its available capacities to survive and grow; judging itself and being judged by others is not relevant to its being. The sense of equality is natural to the infant, as to every human being and we must reclaim our natural entitlement. Equality is a *given*, espoused and highly valued, that is pirated away from many by their circumstances and through the processes of societal rewards and punishments. Paradoxically, society cannot return or bestow equality because that implicitly sustains the superior/inferior dichotomy. The responsibility for reclaiming our innate equality rests upon us.

Since we were all once infants, it's fair to assume that our innate equality still applies. Recently I asked a client to say as an experiment "I'm not as good as you are" and then I said to her "You're not as good as I am." She reported that when she said "I'm not as good as you," she felt sad and discouraged but when I said to her "you're not as good as I am," she was ready to protest and defend herself. We will all defend our equality when it is challenged or attacked from external sources while we are often oblivious to the ways in which we undermine and deny our equality with a barrage of internal attacks. By failing to support her innate sense of equality she was overwhelmed by the problems she faced, thus enfeebling herself all the more.

Separating out *doing* and *being* is an intricate, if not impossible task, for what we do and who we are interpenetrating. Nonetheless, seeing *ourselves* is critical to our ability to problem-solve and feel adequate. To deny that we have not only varying skill levels but also varying aptitudes and abilities is to miss the point. Equality in this context implies relating to one another holistically and not in a segmented fashion comparing skills for skills, looks for looks, tit for tat. Equality is best understood as a psychological posture that establishes an "I-Thou" relationship of mutual respect and esteem. When such a relationship exists the varying levels of skill or talent, size or gender, are irrelevant and our *mutuality* is relevant. Since even skills, talents and looks cannot be measured by agreed upon objective or arbitrary standards, we must look beyond the superficial to discover how we are all truly equal.

Failure to recognize ourselves or another as equal will result in three possible actions: 1) an attempt to protect self or other, 2) an attempt to hide from self or other, or 3) an attack on self or other. Viewing ourselves and others as equal is critical to solving the problems we encounter daily in relationships and in society.

As long as we think about equality in *doing* terms or in relation to aptitudes, talents and skills, we can debate the existence of equality ad infinitum.

A friend of mine who is also a therapist once said to me "I'm as good a therapist as you are." I (who had been her teacher for a number of years) said to her that while I encouraged her learning in every way and supported her as an equal, I assessed my years of experience and therapeutic acumen to be greater than hers. However, whether she agreed or not she was much more likely to develop her talents and skills as a clinician by believing that she and whatever authority she worked with was equal. When we view ourselves and others as equal we are able to assimilate and disseminate information freely and without defense. To objectively establish who is "better" at anything would require an established and agreed up standard.

Equality, conversely, is a subjective standard that we feel on the deepest level. For example, it is fair to assume that an infant that cries out to be fed or comforted experiences itself as equal to the person with the skill and wherewithal to feed and comfort.

Here are some thoughts from the Workbook about equal to begin your reclaiming process.

Equal means that I am not better than or worse than anyone else.

Equal means we are all a part of the whole.

Equal means I can relate to others, no matter how different we are.

Equal means that the person next to me is just as challenged by life as I am.

Equal means my problems are no larger than my abilities.

Creating An Environment Where Healthy Core Beliefs Grow

We all have bright, insightful and even inspiring ideas that we'd like to put into action, but *how* to do that is something "easier said than done." One reason we abandon new ideas and plans is because we don't know how to make changes in our habituated thought and behavior. But by focusing on methods to influence our thought we can gain a degree of objectivity about those patterns and begin to see that in fact they are often little more than "habits." As this realization occurs, we begin to see options we may have overlooked in the past. We've all experienced ourselves as victims while waiting for circumstances to change and things to get better. At some point we realized we'd be better off if we changed rather than continued to wait for the world to change. At the point we decide to change we begin to think of alternatives previously unseen, largely because we weren't looking for them and thought waiting was easier. Finally it wasn't easier anymore. With the new options come new "how-tos." Whenever we experience ourselves as knowing *how* to make a change, change becomes less formidable.

In my clinical practice, in my institutional life and in my personal relationships, my most frequent block to changing from maladaptive functioning to healthy functioning is: "I don't know how!" Since this is the major resistance to change encountered in my experience and in the experience of those I work with, I've elected to present specific exercises to change and positively strengthen core beliefs. When our core beliefs are strong, our energy can be directed toward resolving the problems we encounter.

Gentleness

Through the years, I've witnessed much unnecessary suffering because people have learned new methods of personal and social change and used these new and effective methods in a self-critical manner. I want to caution against such abuses.

As an example, when people learn that parenting deficits contribute directly to the problems they encounter in adult life, they often use the information to blame their parents for their problems. They feel anger and even rage toward their parents, thereby heightening their sense of alienation and separation. This alienation is usually greatest from parents, the very people who, in most cases, helped establish the basic ego strength necessary to recognize the problems in the first place. These insights, which could be extremely useful in strengthening core beliefs, are frequently misused because people fail to make a clear decision about *how* they will use the new information.

If I decide to buy a new and more effective power saw, I should, and probably will, first learn to use it safely. I won't use a new and more effective saw in a reckless manner because I know that it can be as effective at amputating my fingers as it will be in sawing lumber.

What my years as a therapist have brought home to me is that even the best methods of understanding can be, and frequently are, used in a detrimental, hurtful way against one's self or others. This has taught me that it is of critical importance to decide to use new information *for* me and not *against* me.

Gentleness is one of the most powerful components in the learning process and the first and most important ingredient of change is learning to be gentle. The persons who have affected me most deeply and positively have been gentle people. Further, the concepts that I most cherish have come to me in a gentle way. Gentle ideas and gentle people have a way of engaging our unreserved cooperation. When things come to me gently I am eager for more—information and/or experience, and my ability to assimilate and incorporate new information is greatly enhanced. This is not to discount the learning that occurs through harsh encounters. When learning occurs as the result of a harsh encounter we have a tendency to *adapt*, which really amounts to learning "never to do that again," in order to avoid more painful situations rather than learning that is voluntary and characterized by thoughtful options.

Gentleness, as I have experienced it, is sensitive acceptance of ourselves, not syrupy sweetness or condescension. With sensitive acceptance of ourselves, creative ways of dealing with situations eventually occur to us. Gentleness is the lubricant of learning.

We like to be touched, talked to, and engaged gently. When gentleness is the rule rather than the exception, we have a sense of well-being, both physiologically and psychologically, and possess a generally positive attitude toward life. When gentleness is indeed the rule rather than the exception we maintain a deep appreciation of life and experience.

In his book *Transitions*, William Bridges presents three stages of transitions: endings, neutral zones and beginnings. We regularly encounter all these stages in any learning or change process. Each stage is necessary to progress through life, according to Bridges. His emphasis throughout, perhaps more implicitly than explicitly, is that unless we treat ourselves gently, accepting each stage, we prolong our time in one stage or another and the transition may not go well. By gently recognizing what stage we are in, we move through that stage to its natural resolution.

While the power of gentleness could be a topic for much discussion and research, for the time being let me say that *the power of the gentle approach is the most important "how-to" we all possess to build Human Esteem*. Whenever learning and change are not occurring during our process of strengthening Healthy Core Beliefs, the first issue to investigate is whether we are treating ourselves gently.

The Primary Question:
Am I On My Side
or On My Case?

Each of us creates millions of words of internal dialogue a day. These words can have either negative, neutral or positive content. As we begin to notice the content of our internal dialogue, we can shape it so that it is predominantly positive, problem-solving and creative, rather than negative, problem-creating and destructive.

Internal dialogue is the ongoing commentary we make about our daily experiences. We've all spent too much time with someone who comments negatively on every event. This negative dialogue quickly becomes unpleasant to be around and we are likely to want to get away from these kinds of people. Intuitively we can feel the tension created by those who constantly badger and criticize themselves, even if they're not the sort to express it out loud, and this can be just as uncomfortable to be around. Since we don't want to be around them, is it any wonder we'd like to "get away from" ourselves sometimes?

On the other hand, we enjoy being around people who are enjoying themselves. It's fair to assume that their internal dialogue is predominantly positive. It feels good to be in the presence of people who support themselves.

I refer to internal dialogue as either *on my side* (positive commentary) or *on my case* (negative commentary). By this I mean that we either carry on a positive and nurturing internal dialogue (on our side) or we carry on a negative and critical internal dialogue (on our case). When we're on our side we can sustain great amounts of external stress. The extreme illustration of this was demonstrated by the Jews who physically and psychologically survived the concentration camps. In *Man's Search for Meaning*, Dr. Viktor Frankl documents case after case of survival determined by the *attitudinal values* death camp prisoners held.

Too frequently we have little control over the circumstances and situations of our lives. Often we cannot control the stimuli that comes our way. We are, however, in charge of how we relate to ourselves. Our beliefs about ourselves provide internal control over our internal dialogue. If our foundational beliefs are positive and we regularly nourish these beliefs, then we maintain self and Human Esteem. If we become aware of our internal dialogue, realizing that we *can choose* how we relate to ourselves, we'll find that by being gentle and staying on our side we are better able to cope with life. Conversely, if we fail to take responsibility for our internal dialogue and treat ourselves badly, our most frequent reply to life's big and little challenges is likely to be "Don't bother me, I can't cope." Unfortunately, we tend to become critical of ourselves and others at the times when support is what we need most. This occurs, I believe, whenever we do not have Healthy Core Beliefs as the foundation of our esteem. Without Healthy Core Beliefs we will erroneously conclude that when things get tough, the very fact that things *are tough* means there is something intrinsically wrong with us. We will then get on our case rather than gently supporting ourselves by being on our side.

Psychotherapy helps us discover the causal factors behind inadequate or dysfunctional core beliefs. Most psychotherapies focus on understanding the nature of illness or maladaptation. With adequate psychotherapy, we are able to discover where we've made choices and formed beliefs that are not consistent with our nature or conducive to our growth. Through the years I've witnessed people make dramatic changes based on significant insights about early decisions that placed them on wrong life courses. Personally, whenever I am stuck for a prolonged period of time with an issue, I turn to psychotherapy for insight and resolution. I recommend seeking professional help with personal problems just as we seek professional help with automotive or medical problems. Doing one's own psychotherapy, to paraphrase Eric Berne, M.D., is like cutting one's own hair. It can be done, but we make lots of mistakes, it takes a long time and there are places we can't see. Good psychotherapy, to follow the analogy, is like going to a skilled barber and getting the kind of haircut we want the first time.

Psychotherapies tend to focus primarily on pathology, illness and the restoration of healthy functioning. Once we have corrected any historic mistakes we still need a method to assist us in maintaining health and staying on our side. All of the feelings, thoughts and moods of life provide important information that can help with the maintenance of psychological health. Each feeling is a message we need to understand and attend to. If we understand and heed the message, the feeling resolves, but if we misunderstand or ignore the message, the feeling will become more pronounced or distorted. The experience of thirst is a good model in relation to physical well-being. If we're thirsty and get a drink, the thirst is quenched; if we fail to pay attention to our thirst it will become *increasingly* demanding until it becomes all consuming. We *are* thirst and thirsty becomes a major definition of self. This same process occurs with any feeling—if we heed and attend its message it resolves and if we fail to heed and attend the feeling it becomes all consuming.

To say we're depressed is to acknowledge that a feeling is dominating our life and no other feelings, abilities, or ways of being are applicable to us. The feeling becomes us when we fail to ferret out and attend to its message. In the case of depression, we may become completely dysfunctional until we deal adequately with the message our depression brings. On the other hand, once we receive the message and act to correct the factors generating the depression, it will begin to resolve. I've found that by developing a precise understanding of how feelings guide and direct us, we give ourselves the moment-to-moment,

day-to-day support we need. Most of us have only vague defini-
tions of healthy functioning that tend to be characterized either
by an absence of stressful feelings, e.g., anger, frustration, sadness, tension, or presence of pleasant feelings like happiness,
excitement, vitality. I suggest that we be attentive to all feelings
and respect them as the guides of our spirit. Used as guides they
make a bridge with our thinking and can lead to action; feelings
do not indicate that there is something wrong *or right* with us,
they indicate, as the Gestaltists say, "what's up with us."

In the maintenance of psychological health, the primary
question is: *Am I on my side or am I on my case?* Am I making myself feel better or am I making myself feel worse? Am I
providing positive energy for myself by being nurturing, or negative energy by being critical? People who stay on their side are
characterized by their vitality—they are not characterized by
the problems or troubles they encounter in life. People who stay
on their case are characterized by their troubles. Persons who
stay on their case regularly over prolonged periods of time accumulate stress in their systems that eventually shows up as physical disease. Just as the psyche needs positive support to function
creatively, so the physical body needs to be free of psychological stress to function optimally. The barrage of negative internal dialogue causes the biological system to be constantly on
"alert." This overtaxing of the physical body eventually causes a
breakdown of healthy cells.

In psychotherapy, confronting individuals with the right
question is an art. The first rule is to elicit a person's cooperation,

i.e., getting the person on his or her side. This same rule applies to oneself. I will be eager and willing to set the wheels of change in motion when I am on my side. To a large extent, how I treat myself determines how I feel, just as how others treat me determines how I feel about them.

The following illustration demonstrates how early experiences influence the nature of our internal dialogue. George is Jewish and spent the first five years of his life in Nazi Germany. His family survived by being exceedingly quiet, closemouthed and cautious. Though by nature a lively child, the idea that "lively" feelings were "bad" was reinforced by the situation. George rightly concluded as a child that whenever he had a joyous or exuberant feeling, he was in danger. He learned from that tense environment that feeling good/spontaneous meant that he was in danger, and feeling bad/restricted meant that he was safe from catastrophe.

He came to treatment when he was 50, troubled, discouraged, recently divorced and contemplating suicide. As we talked I asked him this simple question, "What do you like about yourself?" While successful in many areas of his life, he was at a loss to say what he liked about himself. He knew well what he did not like. I pointed out that he had a choice between being on his side or on his case. To illustrate this I suggested that he could call himself crazy for coming to see a counselor or he could be grateful to himself for seeking to do something about his pain. That was a choice.

He sat for a moment in silence and then said, "I never realized I had a choice about how I treat myself." He had learned well as a child that to survive he had to stay on his case to restrict his natural spontaneity. That lesson became his style of life.

A short but profound treatment process began for George and several months later he found he was enjoying life with a vitality he had not known before. He learned to confront himself with the key question: *Am I on my case or on my side?* As he regularly noticed how he was treating himself he found that he had more energy available to deal with issues as they came up, energy he had previously used to restrict himself.

As cited earlier, Masterson separates clinical issues (I would add all life issues) into three categories: fate issues, nature issues and nurture issues. Fate and nature issues need to be understood in order to be resolved. Nurture issues involve the ability to arrange environments that feel good and support our health. This is where we have our greatest influence. When we are dealing with nurture issues we must first decide whether we will deal with ourselves negatively or positively.

On our side, we regard ourselves with caring; on our case, we regard ourselves with disdain. "Who among you gives your child a stone when he asks for bread?" When it comes to the way we treat ourselves, all too often the answer to that question is: "I do."

Simply put, positive attention feels good and negative attention feels bad and to a large extent the nature of our internal dialogue determines whether we are feeling good or bad.

Nurture issues most probably exist because of deficits—lack of availability and caring during developmental years. These issues will continue to plague us throughout adult life and until they are examined, we are likely to relate to ourselves in exactly the same manner our parents did to us as we were growing up. If, when our feelings were hurt as a child we were told we were being "too sensitive," then in later years we are likely to be angry with ourselves when we feel hurt and to deny the messages of our feelings lest we be "too sensitive" once again. We've become our own parent, being angry and insensitive to feelings. Again, we are being on our case when we most need us on our side. Since we relate to ourselves far, far more than to anyone else in the world, choosing to be a caring parent to ourselves is critical for our ongoing growth and development.

Current and Past Patterns

We treat ourselves in certain habitual ways. Initially, in order to change those habitual patterns, self-consciousness is required. We need to develop an acute awareness of how we treat ourselves—what we're saying and feeling toward ourselves—in fact, we need to become just as acutely aware of how *we* treat us as how *others* treat us. This decision to *discover* how we really treat ourselves and to get on our side, can leave us feeling a bit stilted and *overly* self-conscious, but it's the best way I've found to begin to break up those old habits and act in new ways that feel better.

In general, we tend to believe that certain external events must happen before we can change. When this is the case, most of us will wait for outside evidence that we are capable, valuable, powerful, lovable and equal before we begin to reinforce and adopt such radical notions about ourselves. If we will just stop for a moment and think about our own lives, we can clearly see how this mistaken belief that we must have external reinforcement *before we will like ourselves* has caused us phenomenal amounts of unnecessary pain. It also consumes vast amounts of time with waiting—for validation, proof or permission. When we recognize that Healthy Core Beliefs can be nourished and quickened by *internal* as well as *external* forces, we eliminate unnecessary waiting and cope with life more efficiently and effectively. "Being on my side" is a "cute" and catchy way of remembering that we need *self-support*, that is, love, appreciation and respect for ourselves, as much as appreciation, love and respect from others.

Our very survival instincts indicate that we all possess a certain amount of "being on our side" tendencies. The question becomes *how much* energy we use "being on our side." The more energy we spend on our side rather than in self-criticism and disparagement, the better. Internal dialogue dictates the quality of day-to-day life. As I mentioned, many people will take new psychological information and use it against themselves. To change the impact of the internal dialogue we must judiciously use new information in a new way. For example, as you read this you can be using this information to be on your case rather than on your side. If your internal dialogue is, "Oh, that's interesting and helpful to know, I will watch for it happening," you are probably on your side.

If you are saying something like, "Damn, that's what I do to myself again and again," you're probably on your case. If by reading this you recognize you're on your case, feel tense, and are saying something that indicates you've goofed yet again, you're still on your case. If you're choosing to be critical of being critical, you are on your case. If you're critical of being critical of being critical, you are on your case *ad infinitum*.

The only way I've found to break this cycle is to shift your response to something like, "Oh, that's how it works, how interesting." Whenever you are on your side, you will experience a feeling of relief. Even in our most painful and difficult moments, we will not feel abandoned because *we* are staying on our side. Being on your case will produce feelings of stress. No matter how sophisticated we are at being self-critical so that we don't sound self-critical *our feelings will let us know* how we are treating ourselves—with a blessing or a curse.

By regularly noticing whether we are on our side or on our case, we can increase the amount of positive support we give ourselves. With greater positive support we become aware of new options for dealing with problems, from personal to social. By choosing to be on our side we cooperate with and enhance our natural instincts to grow and develop harmoniously.

My Technique for Staying on My Side

I carry a picture of myself as a child in my wallet. It is one of those "School Days, 1941-42" pictures of a little boy I know more intimately than any other person in my life. Everywhere I go, he goes, and everywhere I've been, he's been. He's always wanted people to understand him, care for him and cherish him. He's never wanted people to mistreat him. Many times he hasn't known what to do, or precisely what would satisfy him. Many times he's bubbled with enthusiasm, been consumed by curiosity, petrified with fear, overwhelmed with grief, filled with rage, warmed with love. This child that I know most intimately has been through the whole range of human experiences and wants someone to understand, appreciate and care about him at all times.

I carry his picture to remind me of his need and sensitivity. I'm the one who knows him best. I'm with him at all times, and I'm the one he is most free to rely on. He depends on me to treat him well. Unless I pay attention to his feelings, unless I nurture and support him, he is in serious trouble. When I care for him properly, he will get his needs met. When his needs are met, he lives in a state of health, experiencing the world in a relaxed manner.

On the other hand, this boy whose picture I carry will become more and more desperate if I don't pay attention to his needs, wants and feelings. He will feel stress if I ignore or mistreat him over a period of time. He will resort to desperate acts for relief. In the same manner that people who are cut off from contact with others take desperate action to meet their need for human contact, so the boy in me will become desperate if I constantly ignore his needs.

Just as this boy was dependent on parents to pay attention to his feelings and to treat them properly when he was young, so too my feelings as an adult send requests for attention from me. My sense of health and well-being is determined by how I respond to those messages. My choice of being on my side or on my case is critical to my sense of well-being. Since I relate to myself every moment and in every situation of life, it is imperative that I recognize how I am relating to myself, and that I be on my side.

The Buck Starts Here

The recognition that how I relate to myself directly influences what I am willing to give and receive from others is one well worth emphasizing. In other words, *I am not likely to let in from others that which I am not providing myself*, and likewise *I am not adept at giving others what I am not giving myself*. The way I relate to me prepares me internally to give and receive. Until I have an appreciation of myself I will not fully receive another's appreciation. Until I support myself, I will have difficulty receiving another's support. This is an extremely important recognition about human dynamics and will serve to keep the focus of responsibility on us rather than on others. Too often, when problems exist, we feel if others would change, give us what we want or be different in relation to us, then we would be free to change, be happy, get on with our lives. This attitude, which all of us hold to some degree, developed during the early years of our lives when we were quite literally, at the mercy of those around us. In order to get along in the family we adjusted to what they said and the beliefs they held, adapting to them as best we could, even though some of those beliefs and behavioral requirements were inappropriate and inaccurate. When we are grown we may still maintain many of the same beliefs about ourselves and "the way things work," adapting to inadequate and inappropriate attitudes. Until we re-examine our beliefs about ourselves and decide what is true about us we continue to relate to ourselves as we were related to. In this sense we are all victims of our early environments, and, as typical of the victim position, our energy is immobilized and we are enfeebled. We often define ourselves and our world in terms of the belief systems we were raised with and they become self-fulfilling prophecies. "The self-fulfilling prophecy is, in the beginning, a *false* definition of the situation evoking a new behavior which makes the originally false conception come *true... [and] perpetuates a reign of error...for the prophet will cite the actual course of events as proof that he was right from the very beginning.*" (Robert Merton, *Antioch Review*, 8, 193, 1948). Changing the way we relate to ourselves empowers us by allowing recognition of the options and resources that were previously obscured by false information.

Here's a personal example of how this works. As a child I was told I was a slow learner and I believed myself to be less perceptive and bright than the other kids. I learned to make up for this deficiency by using what I called "faking" techniques. These techniques "allowed me" to keep up, passing from grade to grade even though, *as I well knew*, I was not as bright as my friends.

By the time I finished college I had made the dean's list, which I credited not to intelligence but to craftiness. When I went for my Army physical, I refused to contribute a dollar to the pot to bet on the highest intelligence score in our group of 20. To my surprise I scored highest, but I concluded that since they'd given out several tests to prevent cheating, I must have gotten a particularly easy test. I managed to believe this despite the fact that I knew about the standardization of tests. In graduate school I received a full scholarship each year for three years, but credited it to to luck rather than intelligence. "It was a small class," I rationalized.

Toward the end of graduate school, I confided to a friend that, "I sure faked out Professor Graham—he gave me an A." Professor Graham was known as a particularly intelligent and thorough member of the faculty. My friend retorted, "You must be pretty smart to fake out Professor Graham." His comment got through my firmly entrenched beliefs about my intelligence and I began to wonder—"Does it take intelligence to fake someone out? Could it be that I *am* intelligent and not just a good faker?"

Slowly I moved from being on my case about my intelligence and ability to being on my side. When I changed my thinking about my intelligence I also changed my way of relating to myself. I gradually began to notice that I was getting external recognition for my abilities, and I further realized that recognition had always been around in a variety of ways, but I'd never perceived it. I have told this story to many people who've recognized similar processes in themselves. Their issues may have been different, but the process was the same. The way I relate to me determines the way I experience the world relating to me.

Recently a client announced, "I like myself." For the past two-and-a-half years she'd been going through a very arduous divorce, had health problems and serious difficulties with her children. Nothing had resolved: her health was precarious, the divorce was still unresolved and her children still presented problems, but she had made a noticeable shift during the week between our appointments that allowed her to say "I like myself." I could tell she had changed as soon as she walked into the office. Her face was more alive and she seemed to have more energy. I thought at first that one of the problems had resolved but what had occurred was simply that she'd shifted from being on her case because she had problems to being on her side while she dealt with her problems. She faced the same difficulties, but now she was giving herself the acceptance and self-love necessary to recognize that *she* was not one of her problems.

Whenever I want change, the way to begin is to notice how I am relating to me. Am I on my side or on my case?

Self-Confrontation

"Am I on my side or on my case?" is a self-confrontation. Self-confrontation is far and away the most powerful form of confrontation. If someone tells us that we are intelligent, we can deflect it by thinking, "They really don't know me well enough to say that." If someone points out that we are ineffective, we can distort it with the thought, "They really don't understand." "Other" confrontations can always be distorted or deflected by our ability to rationalize, but a "self" confrontation will provoke thought. By thinking about the mistaken notions we have about ourselves, we begin to clarify them. It was at the point that I raised the question "Could it be that I am intelligent and not just a good faker?" that I began to change.

I glibly say that "if criticism were curative, the whole world would be well," but the fact is that criticism from others and from self, no matter how astute, mostly effects *adaptation* (modifications in behavior to avoid future painful situations) and not *change* (new and more effective behavior). Being on our case, or having someone else on our case, invites us to be defensive.

Defensive energy (feeling and acting defensively) is *protective and reactive*. Creative energy is *pro-active and venturing*.

It is vital to recognize the difference between pro-active and re-active action. Re-active responses are similar to our physical reflexes—we react automatically, out of conditioned and habitual patterns with little or no thought about other options or creative solutions to external stimuli/situations. Pro-active responses, on the other hand, are ones that we've thought through and chosen; they incorporate our creativity by using our ability to think as we respond to outside stimuli and involve awareness of our internal experience. When we address a problem in a pro-active manner we're more likely to create a solution that is satisfying to us than when we address a problem in a re-active manner. Re-active problem solving focuses on what we're *against* and pro-active focuses on what we are *for*. We generally cannot determine the stimuli that comes to us but we can always determine our responses to that stimuli. If we're aware that we can determine our responses we're in a pro-active posture; if we lose sight of that awareness, we're in a re-active posture. A life built primarily around reaction becomes a burdensom drudge, responding to one alarm after another with little or no sense of autonomy. A life built around pro-active responses allows us to use our energy to build environments that stand to give us greater and greater autonomy.

The energy generated by self-criticism is almost entirely re-active and will leave us feeling lost and exhausted by the end of the day. By constantly criticizing ourselves we condition ourselves to run our lives out of re-active energy. Conversely, by maintaining a pro-active posture, being on our side, we offer ourselves nurturing and understanding in response to the ups and downs of life. This process will neutralize the negative energy that comes in from the outside world and we're free to capitalize on the positive energy. As we neutralize the negative energy we exercise our autonomy.

Our society and its institutions venerate critical confrontation and tout it as an effective tool for change. On close examination however, critical confrontation is actually one of the less efficient tools for change because it generates re-active (defensive) energy and stifles creativity. Since criticism is inefficient, feels lousy and works poorly, I decided to look for positive, creative processes to facilitate change.

In general, those who come to therapy have usually had any number of people tell them what they really "should" do, with plenty of discussion about everything they are doing "wrong" thrown in for good measure. They are usually in pain and arrive with detailed lists of what is wrong with them. They almost always come after having been on their case; they feel miserable, victimized and are without hope. They report having tried to make changes and may even have experienced initial success, but find they are unable to sustain those changes. Finally, they come for psychotherapy to unscramble the past and discover how that past impinges on the present. While the people coming for therapy do indeed have circumstances and events in their past that need to be unscrambled, the circumstances and events need to be seen as symptoms rather than causes. The cause of their esteem problems is the accustomed practice of self-criticism—being on their case.

John A. Sanford, a Jungian psychologist and author, comments well (*King Saul, The Tragic Hero*, Paulist Press, 1985) on the significance of psychological unscrambling for both the seriously troubled and the general public. He further recognizes that psychological *mis*understandings have far-reaching social and political consequences. "This is why psychology is not just something for people who are troubled and go to a psychotherapist for help; it is enormously important for all of us. Ignorance of ourselves has grievous social and political as well as personal implications. It's especially important that leaders of nations, or other persons in positions of influence, have a marked degree of psychological awareness."

Causes vs. Symptoms

It is very important to make a distinction between *symptoms* and *causes*. My son called the other day to tell me he had car trouble. When I asked him what was wrong he replied, "It's broken." That the car is "broken" is an accurate description of symptoms. It took a mechanic and specific information about those symptoms to discover the cause. The process of psychotherapy tracks symptoms to causes. Once the cause is established, people begin the work necessary to restore their systems to healthy functioning.

When we experience psychological distress, our symptoms call attention to the fact that we are experiencing a "breakdown" of the healthy, comfortable functioning of which we are capable. At the base of this breakdown is a cause. To treat the symptom is like putting a Band-Aid over the site of a boil eruption—it provides temporary protection. To treat the cause is like taking penicillin to fight the infection. While both are necessary in the treatment, one is curative while the other, taken alone, is only a temporary stopgap measure.

A client came to therapy after having been in treatment with another therapist for a long period of time. The presenting problem was that she was feeling a great deal of anxiety about her family and friends' well-being. Her previous therapist had prescribed Valium and she had taken it every day for seven years. The Valium did indeed reduce her anxiety but it treated the symptom and not the cause. I made an agreement with her to stop taking Valium and to search for the cause of the anxiety. In the course of therapy we found that she had always felt those around her were unable to take care of themselves and that she had to take care of them. When she was three years old her father abandoned her family and her mother relied upon her to help make decisions and take care of her little sister. Obviously, she was greatly overtaxed as a child. As we dealt with these basic causes she willingly participated in Gestalt experiences where she relived and resolved ancient impasses. The cause of her anxiety was circumstantially dictated; she had been forced to abandon her own wants and needs in order to take care of her mother's wants and needs. This is identified as a 'situational role reversal' in which she took on the function of the parent (primary provider) even though she was the child (primary receiver). This role reversal evolved into a core belief that she was the primary provider for all the needs of those close to her and that they were not equal to the task of caring for themselves.

The responsibility she felt from this vantage point was enormous because she was not recognizing others' ability to care for themselves and she naturally felt a great deal of anxiety. No amount of treatment of the "symptom" (anxiety) would correct her basic feeling that responsibility for all those close to her rested entirely on her shoulders. Through the resolution of the issue she was able to understand how it came to be that she felt so responsible for the welfare of those close to her as a child and how that projection of the past on the present was a gross distortion of her current situations. As she adjusted her sense of responsibility to correspond with the realities of the current situation, she no longer felt overtaxed and the anxiety symptoms began to resolve. I suggested that when she felt anxious she should confront herself with the awareness that the other person, as well as herself, had problem-solving and care-taking abilities and to remember that she and others/others and she, were equal. As she began to strengthen the Healthy Core Beliefs, the incidents of anxiety dropped off sharply. Treatment of the symptom with Valium merely masked the cause of her anxiety; dealing with the causal issue, and helping her to strengthen her Healthy Core Belief allowed her to be free from constant and incapacitating anxiety.

Human Esteem exists when we recognize that all people are capable, powerful, valuable, lovable and equal. This recognition serves as the foundation we need to solve issues in ourselves, in our relationships and in the world. Thriving Human Esteem allows us to move beyond the estrangement from self and others caused by the shortcomings of family and society. To the extent that Human Esteem exists we are able to heal the ancient hurts that divide us. With our focus on Human Esteem, we are not trapped by an ego-serving psychology, but rather are able to utilize psychological understanding to promote oneness throughout every aspect of life. *"It is the objective of therapy to become one with one's self and at the same time with humanity."* *(Essays on Contemporary Events*, C.J. Jung)

Belief Systems

The healthy function of a belief system is to allow us to organize the information and experience of each moment, thereby making it possible to assimilate and incorporate that new information and experience in a way that won't overwhelm us. Belief systems provide us with psychological equilibrium—they are frames of references that tell us how to react to life—who we are and what to do. As a way of looking at the profound effect our belief systems have on our lives, I'd like to look at some of the beliefs we hold about problems and problem-solving.

As children, when things went badly, many of us were confronted with accusations like "who did this?" and "why did you do that?" So we learned that in the face of problems, we should look for a person to "blame." Children with this belief system will become adults with a strong tendency to blame self or others when they encounter difficulties. As long as we believe that it's someone's *fault* when things go wrong, we will search for someone to blame—often ourselves—and expend vast quantities of energy on feelings of anger, guilt, frustration, etc. instead of using that energy to search for a solution.

In the process of rewriting this section, we spent nearly four hours working and reworking these few paragraphs to get them down just right and had finally succeeded. The next day I called up the page and discovered that all the work we'd done had been lost. It crossed my mind to blame Thomas who kept telephoning and asking me to hurry, or I could blame technology (always a favorite), or I could blame myself for letting Thomas rush me or for being too careless to notice that the disk was too full to accommodate the new information. The belief I immediately encountered, after the immediate shock of pain at the loss and anger at having to start anew subsided, was that we'd never be able to recapture the clarity and essence of the thoughts we'd finally achieved and that whatever we came up with would be a sorry substitute. *"It's my fault* (I should have been more careful), *it's going to hurt* (why am I even putting myself through this torture) *and it's going to last* (I'll never reach an acceptable solution and these paragraphs will be bad forever) pretty much sums up my position at this moment. The question becomes, will I choose to proceed, one step at a time, toward solving the problem, despite the counter-productive belief outlined above, or will I let my frustration and sense of hopelessness prevail. Clearly, unless I choose to give up entirely on this portion of the book, a more realistic and encouraging belief system is called for. I need to believe that problems are a *natural part of life* (most aren't anyone's "fault"); they can be overcome (they won't last forever) and taking the first steps of the solution are the most painful. With this belief system operative I am able to assimilate the sense of loss and frustration I felt and, rather than staying stuck there, will feel up to the task at hand: starting over again. The point is not to deny the feelings of pain and anger, but to move beyond them. Things go wrong from time to time for everyone and, if we wish to treat ourselves in a responsible manner, our job is to move toward understanding and correcting whatever went wrong (even as we speak, I've moved files and made more room on this disk) so that we can move ahead with our lives. By solving problems as they arise, life always has the promise of authentic discovery while rehashing what when wrong and why keeps us stuck in melodrama.

Changing a belief system is not easy because it always involves risk to move from a known to an unknown, even when the "known" has proven to be dysfunctional. The fact is, once we've reached the point where we are ready to start looking for a new way of being and believing, it is probably because we intuitively recognize that the risk is more likely to bring gain than loss. At the moment of abandoning our old, comfortable beliefs, we're probably not feeling like we've just gotten hold of a winning lottery ticket, but that's part of the trick of changing old beliefs. They generally have built into them the idea that they are the only ones that will work and all others are doomed to failure. A new, healthier belief system would include the idea that taking a risk is as likely to result in a gain as a loss, and as everybody says about the lottery, "somebody's got to win."

Letting go of old beliefs is difficult in the same way that New Year's resolutions are difficult—resolutions concentrate our focus on what we are losing rather than on the potential gain from our effort. This stumbling block is best circumvented by concentrating on the new way we will feel and live once we have accomplished certain changes. It's well known that once we no longer smoke, we will have increased energy and vitality; concentrating on what a difference this vitality will make in our lives is quite different from concentrating on quitting smoking. We can concentrate on *giving up* (smoking) or we can concentrate on *taking up* (vitality).

Creating a new known is similar to the process of obtaining an education. First we decide what we want and then go about the process of accumulating the information necessary to procure that want (e.g., a degree in anthropology). Creating a new known means deciding on what we want and systematically going about acquiring it.

Just as the developing child relates to role models and ego ideals as a way to shape their developing personality, so adults who are operating on a belief system that does not provide a sense of fulfillment need to focus on the beliefs that will support them to become who and what they want to be. This kind of focus is routine in the attainment of work-related, relational and personal achievement goals, yet we do not routinely focus on the attainment of new, more fulfilling personal beliefs, goals and models in our psychological/spiritual development. Most of us hold the belief that surrounding ourselves with new and more elaborate technological advances will lead to feelings of satisfaction. Alternatively, if we believed that responding to and being guided by what "inspires" us will lead to feelings of satisfaction, we would run our lives much differently. We are inspired by Mother Theresa and we are encumbered by our Cuisinarts, yet commonly-held beliefs support the idea that one more labor-saving device will provide us with our longed-for sense of fulfillment. Changing belief systems is one way that we can escape the bondage of Madison Avenue; consumer-oriented fulfillment that always falls so short of the mark. Before we will abandon a commonly held and well-reinforced belief, we must decide on, affirm and support a belief that resonates with our own "true self," after thoughtful consideration of what will truly lead us to a sense of fulfillment. Manifesting our true self comes through allowing ourselves to be guided by those things which deeply inspire us.

Belief systems can be changed quickly and finally when the right circumstances confront us. For many years, dealing with authority figures was troublesome for me. Each time I failed to confront someone in authority, I would be unhappy with myself (on my case). Year after year, event after event went by and I continued to repeat what I considered "wimpy" behavior. While I was taking an oral exam for a teaching credential that was very important to me, one of the examiners said that for her the real determinant of passing or failing candidates was whether they believed in themselves sufficiently to confront the examiners as well as the people they would be training. She went on to say that clear confrontations told her a candidate thought of himself or herself as a peer of the members of the examining board. I immediately recognized that I did indeed consider myself a peer of the examining group and as I realized this, I also recognized that the behavior in myself that I didn't like was based on an archaic belief that other people would ridicule me if I expressed thoughts and opinions that challenged them.

Although this belief, which had once provided me some degree of safety by keeping me out of trouble with my stepfather(s), was now totally inappropriate, it nevertheless still controlled me in situations like this examination. Though I had generally come to believe myself to be equal to others and safe to express my opinion, I had not consciously applied this belief to situations like this where certain individuals had greater "authority" than I. My new known became the belief that I was equal as a person and free to confront whenever I deemed it appropriate. Since then I have operated on a new and assertive belief in the face of authority and have shifted from passive (wimpy) confrontation to assertive, equal confrontation. This relatively quick shift exemplifies how the change of a belief system can be liberating and sometimes involve nothing more than stopping to ask ourselves, in difficult situations, what belief our actions are based upon and what our current beliefs actually are.

Our failure to flow and change, recognized as resistance, must be respected. Resistance provides the human organism with the positive qualities of safety and protection, however, and it is a big however, resistance literally forces us to deal with the same problems over and over, *until we get it right.*

To move beyond resistance we must learn to respect the message sent through the experience of resistance and at the same time confront ourselves in such a way that we don't stimulate greater resistance. I have found only one intervention truly effective in getting beyond our resistances: *a self-confrontation gently posed*. This is a delicate operation and needs to be done with great gentleness and sensitivity.

Self-Confrontation

I find the most effective and gentle form of self-confrontation occurs when we question our belief systems. "Am I willing to believe...?" as a form of self-confrontation is respectful of previous beliefs, gentle in tone and supportive of personal autonomy. I believe that these three qualities—respect for previous beliefs, gentleness of tone and support for personal autonomy— are hallmarks of healthy caring. It is well documented throughout modern developmental psychology that when healthy caring is available, the child is free to follow its natural cycle of exploring the universe, returning to report, receiving reassurance and then venturing out again. These are the characteristics of the rapprochement stage that is critical to separation and individuation in human development. In the best of all possible worlds, were the process of separation and individuation allowed to complete itself successfully, Healthy Core Beliefs would quite naturally be well established in everyone's psyche. Since a child is likely to incorporate internal dialogue based on the actual experiences of childhood, the criteria for effective self-confrontation that facilitates completion of developmental tasks and produces Healthy Core Beliefs, needs to be consistent with the same models of parenting known to produce healthy individuals. Words, tone and posture are critically important. I've noticed that I will listen carefully and think deeply about what others have to say if, in their contact with me, they offer respect, gentleness and recognition of my autonomy. Therefore to confront myself effectively, it is important that I use those same methods *as I relate to me*.

Respect, gentleness and recognition of autonomy are powerful tools with which to build new beliefs that allow me to live harmoniously within myself, in relationships and in the institutions and structures of society, yet giving ourselves respect and gentleness is not automatic and we therefore must learn to monitor our internal dialogue.

When two people are attempting to resolve an issue and each gets on their own case in the process, the stage is set for a molehill becoming a mountain; it's also relatively certain that everybody's feelings will get hurt. I watched this happening recently between a friend and her father and later asked if she'd like to hear my description of their interaction. She said she would, because both of them had ended up feeling badly, she felt like she'd blown it and though she didn't really know *what* had happened, she knew *something* bad had happened. Her father, a carpenter, had come over to help with a building project and immediately told her his solution to the problem. She began to ask him questions about certain details of his solution so that she'd understand more about the whole situation.

He quickly clammed up and she immediately assumed that he was angry and asked him why he was getting mad. This pattern had gone on for years—he would end up feeling hurt and she would end up feeling misunderstood and still in the dark. As we talked about the differences between them, I pointed out that her father's position as a construction superintendent had always been to take charge and make things happen. Detailed explanations of his solutions were not part of his repertoire. In her attempts to gain an understanding for herself with questions, it seemed to me that he began to think she didn't trust him to take care of her. Instead of getting what he wanted, which was appreciation, and perhaps a bit of adoration, she seemed to be giving him the third degree and he felt hurt. When he felt hurt, she assumed he was angry at her and began to feel inadequate. They both walked away unfulfilled and frustrated. I thought they had missed another chance for the closeness they both wanted and were blaming themselves for the "failure." I believe that the primary reason we do things together is to share the whole range of caring feelings we have for one another and whenever we fail to do so we are likely to get on our case rather than think through what went wrong and figure out a better way to go about it next time.

As we talked through the situation, she began to understand his idiosyncratic style, how important it was for him to be able to "take care" of her and that her questioning could be seen as not trusting his abilities. I suggested that the next time she wanted additional information, she show her appreciation *first, then* ask for explanations of his plan, and see if that worked better. With this new slant on the situation, she relaxed visibly because she saw the possibility of solving this long-standing problem. She moved into being on her side as she saw how to let him know that she was on his side.

"Am I willing to believe...?" is also an effective self-confrontation because by posing such a question, we respect the old belief system (known) while applying our current thought to build a new belief system *(a new and more valid known)*. It's important to remember that old beliefs about ourselves are based on survival instincts and decisions about what we must do to survive formed while our minds were not fully developed. Some of these beliefs involve the decisions of a six-month-old mind, some a six-year-old mind and some a 16-year-old mind. Once a belief system is established, we use it automatically until it is replaced by an updated system, even if it fails to be fully adequate or to reflect our current situation and abilities. We all function with belief systems of ancient origin as well as contemporary origin. When we experience ourselves as unable to make life work, we need to know the belief system that is operative as well as understand the specific problem we encounter.

None of us would think it foolish to take a class in financial management if we were continually experiencing financial problems. We would assume that if we had a better understanding we could function more competently. However, when we're having problems with our ability to maintain anything from a friendship to a healthy, rewarding sex life, we often resist the need for a new cognitive understanding. Instead of assuming we need a better understanding, we frequently jump to the conclusion that there is something basically *wrong* with us because we have a problem. The result is: when we have a problem we get on our *case* at a time when we most need to be on our *side*.

Similar life problems are perpetuated year after year when we do not change our belief systems. As long as old belief systems color our interpretation of reality, we are caught in a trap of our own making.

Core Beliefs

Core beliefs form the foundation of belief systems. A belief creates a system of self-support which allows us to organize and assimilate experiences. Without belief systems we would be overwhelmed by a chaotic flood of incoming information. We often have beliefs that are adequate for organizing our world, but which are *inadequate* for healthy, happy functioning. As an example, a core belief taught by the Judeo-Christian tradition is the commandment, "You shall love the Lord your God with all your heart, and with all you mind; and your neighbor as yourself." Most believers will readily admit their failure to live up to this commandment. Their failure comes, I believe, because the "self-love" foundation necessary for "other" love is never directly and thoroughly addressed, much less supported. The believers who focus only on loving neighbor or God generally judge themselves as falling short of this basic precept of their faith and experience the attendant self-criticism. When people build adequate core beliefs about self-love, they will be able to perform their devotion and service in a way they will judge as satisfactory—"living up to" this most basic commandment.

We will now turn to a discussion of Healthy Core Beliefs. I trust that you will have the wisdom to use this information I am presenting gently. The self-confronting questions are:

1. *Right now*, am I on my side or on my case?
2. *Right now*, am I willing to believe that I am: a capable human; a powerful human; a valuable human; a lovable human; and that I and all other humans are equal?

Groucho Marx once said, "I wouldn't belong to any club that would have me as a member." When we stop to think about why this strikes us as funny, we realize it's because we find in it a familiar paradox—we often trap ourselves much the same way Groucho does. Most of us hold certain other people in higher esteem than ourselves. Like Groucho and his sought-after club, if and when we gain acceptance by these others, rather than feeling pleased and proud, we conclude that our high regard for them must have been a mistake.

At the heart of every human problem are issues of esteem. Human beings solve very complex and intricate dilemmas when they believe in themselves and support their basic value and abilities, but when such support is not present, the most elementary problems stymie us. I recently heard a speech by the man who built the first airplane able to fly two miles with only human power. He was inspired to build the plane after reading that there was a $100,000 prize posted for anyone who could accomplish this feat. He was also spurred on by the fact that he was $100,000 in debt. The prize had been posted for 50 years and aeronautical engineers had assumed it was impossible to build such a craft. Fortunately, he was not an aeronautical engineer and did not know that it was impossible. He did know enough about aerodynamics to be able to say to himself: "I can do that—all I need is a wide enough wingspan." And so he did it. In this instance, his assessment of himself proved crucial to accomplishing the task at hand. Without sufficient belief in himself and his abilities, he would never have undertaken such an "impossible" feat. Time and time again I've seen that when people believe in themselves and in each other and mutual esteem abounds, human beings find ways of dealing creatively and nonviolently with life problems. Another way of saying this is: When I experience myself as loving another, the resolution of differences is usually not too difficult. If it is difficult, it is not intolerably hard to live with whatever differences exist. When love exists my esteem of self and others is healthy and healing.

When Healthy Core Beliefs make up the foundation of our self-concept we will relate to one another with Human Esteem. Human Esteem needs to be firmly rooted in our individual psyches before we will seek to peacefully negotiate our personal, relational and social conflicts.

I began recognizing the existence of Healthy Core Beliefs through investigation and observation of people working on life issues in therapy. As a parent, I wondered what essential beliefs I wanted my children to hold about themselves and others as they moved into the world on their own. As a psychotherapist, most of my clients' greatest difficulties came from their inability to believe in themselves. I worked with them as they searched for ways to express their true nature and to become free to believe in themselves. As a clergyman, I wondered what Healthy Core Beliefs my congregants needed to support themselves and one another in order to live in peace and harmony, and to cope with the challenges that often accompany attempts to achieve idealistic goals. And, as an individual searching for personal stability, I wondered what psychological foundations I needed to live and work peacefully and effectively. I also asked myself what Healthy Core Beliefs human beings need in order to recognize that they are citizens of the world. What did we need to believe about ourselves and each other to heighten our sense of common humanity and to be prepared to resolve the problems of our age?

The challenge of this multi-dimensional questioning, coupled with my belief that solutions, when discovered, were simple rather than complex, culminated in the five Healthy Core Beliefs that I present as essential to Human Esteem. I have found that individuals in whom these core beliefs are well-established are able to maintain a strong sense of their own autonomy and are also less likely to feel like they are victims. Instead, people who believe in themselves take "what is" in stride—coping with, altering where possible and accepting where impossible, the facts of their lives. Again, Viktor Frankl, who survived the horrors of the Nazi regime without losing his sense of personal autonomy, comes to mind. He managed this by remaining constantly aware that he was always in charge of his attitude, regardless of the circumstances in which he found himself. He recognized that *attitudinal values* were the mark of his humanness—not circumstantial conditions or the treatment he received from others.

Dr. Frankl reported that throughout his concentration camp experience he kept Nietzsche's insight close to his heart: "He who has a *why* for living can endure almost any *how*." By constantly keeping his focus on the *why* of his life rather than the *how*, he was better equipped to survive the loss of his loved ones, the deaths of his friends, the degradation of imprisonment and apparent hopelessness. Frankl's example is testimony to how healthy beliefs sustain us.

Healthy Core Beliefs are also attitudinal values. Ideally, Healthy Core Beliefs would be regularly taught and reinforced in children as they progress through normal developmental stages. My friend, colleague, and mentor Robert D. Phillips, M.D. has skillfully outlined the basic "ascription messages" a child needs to receive during their developmental stages. These ascription messages are:

1. survive 2. take care of yourself 3. be competent 4. be close to others 5. learn by trial and error 6. have fun 7. take care of others appropriately 8. think for yourself 9. feel what you feel

When the developing child receives healthy ascription messages, the adult develops beliefs about self and others that support autonomy. In Phillips' words, "The autonomous system... is the repository of psychological liveliness and of a firm sense of self in the world, deriving from the balanced interplay of the organism and the environment. The values are liberal and participatory and the view is cosmic. The attributes of the autonomous system are awareness, spontaneity, gracefulness and intimacy...in the here and now." The ascription program a child receives from its parents determines which beliefs are nourished and which are not. Many of us go through the developmental stages with insufficient nourishment, teaching and support to form Healthy Core Beliefs, resulting in problems of esteem (of self and/or others).

When problems of esteem exist, they come to our attention most notably in close, intimate relationships. When this occurs we have a tendency to focus on the difficulties in the relationship or attack the other person's character rather than to address personal core belief issues.

For many years it was difficult for me to receive constructive criticism from my wife about the training events I led. In each argument about this, I finally resorted to saying, "I'm sure you could have done it better than I did" or "Why don't you just take charge of everything." She tried to explain that she was only talking about a few minor points on which I could improve and I'd become angry, defensive and reject the information. After this had disturbed our relationship for a number of years, we finally came to the agreement that she would not, under any circumstances, give me feedback for at least two days after a workshop. She was very faithful to the agreement but during that time I found that I'd imagine her responses, feeling alienated from her even though she wasn't critiquing my performance.

As I began to realize my problem and finally deal with my own sense of inadequacy and strengthen my healthy core beliefs, I projected less and less negative commentary onto her and experienced more and more support from her. One day about two years after we made this agreement, she forgot herself and violated our pact. Teasingly, I told her she could take her opinions and "go suck eggs." We began laughing and on the way home I told her that now she could give me her feedback spontaneously because I'd finally recognized and dealt with my own issues. Not infrequently our problems with intimacy are problems within ourselves, between *us and us*, not between us and another. It is only when we confront ourselves, respectfully, gently and supportively, that we get the kind of support that sets the stage for true intimacy with another. It is in close relationships that many of our own difficulties capture our attention most noticeably, and if we look closely at underlying causes we will usually find specific Healthy Core Beliefs are at issue.

Fight and Flight

At the points where our esteem of self or others lacks the support offered by Healthy Core Beliefs, we tend to abandon our creative and uniquely human capacities, resorting to primitive, animal-like defenses. Creative, human capacities are best characterized by non-violent resolution of problems. Animal-like defense capacities are best characterized by responses programmed into us through millions of years of evolution in "jungle environments." When we use these responses as problem-solving methods, the problem may temporarily vanish, but in all likelihood it will turn up again and again in different forms. When we use archaic responses repeatedly, we are actually reinforcing our primitive responses, and slowly come to feel that we're incapable of actually *resolving* certain problems effectively.

These primitive animal-like defenses are referred to as *fight* and *flight* and do not, in fact, solve problems. If I solve a problem by avoiding it (flight) the problem usually lingers in my mind and turns up again in a different form or in a new situation. It's like trying to hide from a bill collector. When I solve a problem by force (fighting), I'm likely to act in a destructive manner—in addition to not really solving the problem. This results in additional new sources of tension: I may dislike myself for my "bad" behavior, and I may fear retaliation. All these feelings and actions eventually erode my self-esteem.

When we fight and lose, our internal dialogue will probably be negative and self-critical, although our need for support grows as our discomfort increases. If we win, the momentary adrenalin rush that accompanies victory is frequently followed by self-doubting thoughts like: "Will I be strong enough or shrewd enough to win next time?" It is only when I understand the cause of the problem and work to find a way to truly resolve it that I find a suitable solution.

Fleeing doesn't create solutions either. When we run away from our problems we generally use the occasion to get on our case. Our internal dialogue is filled with self-disparaging remarks like: "I'm such a coward, a real chicken"; or "A real man/woman would have stood up to that situation." The list of self-disparaging comments is lengthy. Just as in the aftermath of the fight method, when our internal dialogue is filled with negative self-commentary, our need for support grows and feelings of personal discomfort increase. Chances are these feelings will start us thinking about fight or flight and the cycle will be repeated once again.

Resolution

Resolution is a third option that leads to *solutions*, but it is often neglected in our problem-solving processes. Physiologically, resolution is the final stage in the healing process. When tissue is traumatized and cells are damaged and destroyed, the adrenocorticotropic hormone (ACTH) produced by the pituitary gland activates the body's defense system. ACTH activates a natural sealing-off of the damaged areas with fluid. This is characterized by swelling. Then, through capillary action, blood cells carry the dead tissue away from the sealed-off area and new cells replace the dead tissue. This process is easily seen in a bruise. Trauma is followed by swelling, discoloration, removal of damaged or dead cells and then the growth of new, healthy cells—resolution. During the process it is possible to actually watch healing occur. A bruise will become lighter day by day until the area returns to normal.

Resolution is also recognized as the completion stage in the human sexual response cycle as identified by Drs. Masters and Johnson. These researchers isolated and identified the four phases of the human sexual response cycle: excitation, plateau, orgasm and resolution. Each phase has its unique characteristics and normal, healthy biological function: charging and discharging. It's important to note that the cycle ends in resolution. Resolution completes the cycle and without it, the process fails to provide its natural organismic balancing.

In the learning process there is a fluctuation between what is known and unknown. We venture out into the new, unknown territory, creating stress in our system, and then return to a known, where we relax and assimilate the new information. The process takes us back and forth between a state of stress and relaxation. Assimilation of new information occurs in the relaxed state and learning is complete when we reach resolution. With each successful sequence we develop a new known out of a previous unknown—thus stress and relaxation, in proper proportions, resolve in learning.

These examples illustrate that resolution is the process by which we *heal the body, restore organismic balance* and *assimilate new experiences*. The state of non-resolution (stress), whether it be over a very small issue or a very large one, keeps us feeling up in the air, distracted, uneasy, and unable to fully focus on the present because we're still preoccupied with the unfinished business of the past. The larger the issue we're grappling with, the more of our being is consumed by this disturbance in our equilibrium. As closure, or resolution occurs, we have an emotionally corrective experience that allows us to assimilate the emotional and cognitive information gained in the experience, making us ready for what's up next in life. The next event could be exciting, frustrating, relaxing, painful—we don't know—but we will be in the present rather than the past, and in the present, "one thing follows another."

When things stop following one another, we are most likely focusing on the past or the future and those are two major ways we obstruct change, movement and progress. As we adequately support our Healthy Core Beliefs, our focus remains in the present where life is actually lived. We stay with the process of resolution in the present by asking "Am I willing to believe _____ (fill in *your own* Healthy Core Belief) right now?" or "Am I willing to believe that I am a capable, powerful, valuable, lovable and equal person?" instead of something like "I am an *inadequate, uncreative, boring, nerdy, bubble-headed drip* (or *all of the above*). When resolution is completed, the organism strikes a natural balance called health.

Problems and Resolution

When a problem is resolved, we feel a sense of achievement and are confident that if a similar problem arises again, we will be able to solve it. Life becomes more of an adventure and less like a melodrama when resolution is our method of problem-solving. A long-term friend used to call periodically and ask to get together "for a talk." I came to know this kind of talk meant that a lengthy tale of woe would be recited about how difficult his life was and how everyone misunderstood him. These "talks" would usually go on for about two hours. I would offer him some advice, lend him some money, and he would leave with his problems apparently resolved. Once after this happened, I began to notice that these encounters all had a very similar feel of melodrama about them. I thought about the similarities over the years and recognized that each episode had several things in common. He would enter in great distress, there would be a recital of how others had misunderstood him and then after we had talked I would learn that he was desperate for money. I then lent him money which he regularly repaid. I also realized that I never heard if my advice had helped and I never heard about problems that required any solution other than money. Once I saw the pattern clearly, I decided to call and tell him that I'd always be available to help if I could when he needed money and to just let me know. The melodrama ceased at that point and from then on when a need arose he made a direct request for money in a very businesslike fashion.

I knew this particular melodrama very well because it was exactly the same procedure he had gone through with his father when he was a child. Most of our melodramas are based on protocols we learned as children. In this case resolution occurred by making explicit my willingness to help when I could which allowed us to feel good about our friendship rather than confused by the melodramatic nature of our previous encounters. The path to resolution is frequently the discovery of a process with which to deal with problems and *in*frequently the discovery of a once-and-for-all solution.

To achieve resolution we must be on our side throughout the problem-solving process. Resolution is never *easily* accomplished of course, because if we knew the solution in the first place, we wouldn't have a *problem* on our hands. To effectively resolve a problem we must summon our creative energies, apply them to the problem, and above all, support ourselves each step of the way with positive internal dialogue (being on our side). We need to intentionally support our adult selves in the same way we were supported and encouraged as children when we were attempting something new—"That's right..." and "Now you've got it…" are familiar words of encouragement. Choose your own and use them generously.

Creativity involves risk-taking and to access our creative energies for problem-solving, we first need to believe in our own abilities to make life better. Healthy Core Beliefs provide the internal psychological support necessary to courageously address the problems we face. The day won't come when we don't have problems to resolve; our best choice is to support ourselves in such a way that we will feel free to take creative risks. Problem-solving, I believe, is best seen as an unavoidable, life-long learning process—and one that can be challenging and interesting rather than just something to endure.

Healthy Core Beliefs provide the support necessary for us to think we can win when problem-solving is necessary. Just as we won't fight unless we believe we're capable of winning and we won't flee unless we either believe that we're capable of getting away or have absolutely no other choice, so we will not organize our energies for resolution unless we believe we have the capacity to succeed. Core beliefs that support Human Esteem allow us to seek resolution when confronted with difficulties.

Problems and Issues

When Healthy Core Beliefs form the foundation of our esteem, we experience problems as issues to be resolved rather than as *Problems* with a capital "P." We need only sit in on a therapy group for a short time to realize that most everyone's problems are very similar. This is actually a very heartening discovery because it means that our problems are not the source of our specialness and because it's always a great relief to discover that "we're not the only one." One thing I've discovered that all people have in common is the desire to be special; frequently we use our problems as a way to fulfill this universal desire. When problems are no longer the source of our specialness, we are free to refocus our energy in a more interesting and productive search for the unique aspects of our personal character.

This search begins when we accept and support our true selves and *allow* our specialness to emerge. I use the word *emerge* very deliberately here. Specialness is something that emerges as we physically develop, psychologically mature and chronologically advance through life's cycles. In each transition, specialness emerges naturally when we are well supported (on our side). Consequently, the more attention and nourishment we give to our Healthy Core Beliefs, the easier it is for our true, inner core to emerge and have the chance to *be* and *do* in the world.

Erik Erikson has outlined the stages of life as he sees them in *The Life Cycle Completed* (W.W. Norton & Co., New York, 1982):

Stage	Healthy Resolution	Resolution Issue
Infancy	Hope	Basic Trust vs. Basic Mistrust
Early Childhood	Will	Autonomy vs. Shame/Doubt
Play	Purpose	Initiative vs. Guilt
School Age	Competence	Industry vs. Inferiority
Adolescent	Fidelity	Identity vs. Identity Confusion
Young Adult	Love	Intimacy vs. Isolation
Adulthood	Care	Generativity vs. Stagnation
Old Age	Wisdom	Integrity vs. Despair, Disgust

In these stages he notes both healthy and pathological development for each age. It is the availability of support and nurture which allows for a healthy progression through each stage. Whenever we use our problems to make us special, we are stuck and restrict our natural, emerging selves. Rather than believing there is a way to overcome and emerge stronger and happier from whatever dilemma we are in (healthy resolution of the psychological crisis), we become bogged down with the "baggage" of the past and may never discover the strengths and talents we possess. The more we think of ourselves as special because of certain problems we have, the less likely we are to see ourselves as able to deal effectively with life in the present.

A friend of mine had spent much of her life struggling with her inability to like herself. That sense of unacceptableness centered around the "legitimacy" of her conception. Her parents had neglected to follow the socially approved timetable in conceiving her. She dubbed herself illegitimate at best and bastard at worst. In addition to personally induced problems, she had the socially induced problems of being black and poor in the United States. To this she added the feeling that she was responsible for being conceived in an "unacceptable" manner. Since there was nothing she could do to amend the circumstances of her conception or pigmentation, she saw herself as a victim. The best she could hope for was to appreciate herself "in spite" of who she thought she *really* was.

She told her story in a treatment group and no one accepted the "logic" that she was responsible for the circumstances of her conception. They argued that what her parents did in relation to society's expectations and prejudices had no bearing on her acceptability. At this point she became confused because she had "told all" and the group refused to see her as unacceptable *or* as a helpless victim.

I asked her to imagine her parents in front of her and tell them she was not responsible for her conception. The impact of this thought, stated overtly for the first time, overwhelmed her with emotion. She spent a few moments in a mixture of sadness and joy. As the sadness and tears subsided, she came to see that her parents had never consciously made her responsible for their lovemaking. She turned to the others of the group and said joyfully, "I'm not responsible for my creation—only my life—and I can handle that." Her life did not instantly become problem-free, but when she began to change the way she thought about and treated herself, life changed dramatically for the better. She was able to cope with the issues of her life and think of herself as equal to the people she met.

A few months after this experience she accompanied me to a workshop at a university in another city. Of the 30 people assembled, at least half had graduate degrees and several were psychologists and psychiatrists from other countries. During the workshop, one of the foreign psychiatrists confessed that deep down, he felt like a fraud and unacceptable despite the fact that he was very successful and prominent in his community. He thought of himself as different from and "less than" others because he was illegitimate. My friend from the ghetto leaned over to me and whispered, "The doctor has my problem, and here all these years I thought that was what made me 'special.'"

I asked the psychiatrist to perform the same exercise with his parents visualized before him. A year after the therapeutic experience, he wrote saying that many people in his country were now getting well because while he'd previously viewed his problem as irreversible and unsolvable, he now recognized that he'd unconsciously projected that view onto many of his clients. Of course he could not reverse the facts of his birth, but he realized that he need not view those facts as "a problem" and saw that thinking about them differently could mean a radical change in how he perceived himself, others and life. The same could be true for his clients. Viewing facts of the past as real circumstances is important to good mental health, but is quite different from seeing them as problems. This subtle shift in perspective can change the way we approach everything.

These examples illustrate what happens to people when they cease to use their problems to make themselves special, offer themselves adequate support and operate on Healthy Core Beliefs. The events described above happened over fifteen years ago. I've maintained contact with both and can report that they have a sense of belonging and a renewed optimism since they stopped making themselves "special" because of fate issues. By using a fate issue to define ourselves we unconsciously place ourselves in a victim position.

Button, Button,
Who's Got the Button?

One further distinction that needs to be made is to clearly determine just where the issue/problem resides. An issue/problem exists primarily in one of two places: internally, between "me and me," or externally, between me and the environment. In the above example, both people identified their problem as being between them and their environment. No amount of achievement (or self-reprobation) could ever lay the problem to rest. It was only when they looked for a solution between "them and them" that their hurts could finally be healed. One of the early games Eric Berne identified is "If it weren't for you." In this game, couples (anyone can play, but primary relationships are particularly fertile ground for this one) spend their lives not doing what they really want to and using the other person as an excuse—"I could do _____ , if it weren't for you." If the spouse becomes unavailable as a scapegoat (death, divorce, unwillingness to take the blame), it can become painfully clear that no one was stopping them but themselves. The issue is between them and them. It is imperative that we determine where the issue/problem resides before seeking to resolve it. If a problem is actually between "me and me" and I address it as an issue primarily between "me and you," not only won't the problem get resolved, it may grow substantially worse.

Our own core beliefs need to be checked out first whenever we experience an *issue* becoming a *problem*. Whether that issue/problem is perceived as being between "us and us" or between us and someone or something in the environment, we need to engage in a systematic process to monitor our core beliefs. Here is a process for doing this:

First. Ask which of the five core beliefs the issue/problem might relate to: Capable? Powerful? Valuable? Lovable? Equal? Your intuitive response will allow you to proceed to the second question.

Second. Ask this question: Am I willing to believe, *right now*, that I am _____ ? (Put your intuitive response in the blank.)

If we answer "yes" to the second question in relation to the current issue/problem, we can begin to focus on *what to do now to move this problem to resolution* rather than *how bad it is* that I have this problem.

If we answer "no," and are unwilling to believe that we are capable, powerful, valuable, lovable or equal, we have established that we must first strengthen a core belief before we can deal with the issue/problem. Here is an example of this process:

Recently I was feeling depressed as I drove to work. I reviewed the issues I was dealing with: financial problems within the

institution for which I work; my wife's grave illness and a heav-
ily committed activity schedule for the day. All of these issues
and more were racing through my mind. This was my list on this
particular morning and it is a fairly typical list of the activities
and issues that fill our lives. We always have numerous items
on our "lists." Sometimes we're able to manage the issues better
than other times. When we find ourselves feeling emotionally
"out of balance" we need to track down the cause.

I asked myself: Am I willing to believe I am a capable
human? Yes.

Am I willing to believe I am a powerful human? Yes.

Am I willing to believe I am a valuable human? No automatic 'yes' was forthcoming.

Am I willing to believe I am a lovable human? Yes.

Am I willing to believe I am an equal human? Yes.

As I thought about this, I recognized that all the issues I
faced were primarily focused on other people's needs. My personal time, space and needs were taking a back seat. Apparently
I needed to stimulate, nourish and strengthen my core belief
about my *value*. I drove on to work repeating the question "Am I
willing to believe that I am valuable?" Through the day I raised
the same question several times. As I drove home I found myself
making plans for a creative and exciting gathering—something I wanted to have "just for me." I was no longer depressed.

The depressed feeling was a healthy signal that I was
not balancing my time and energy well—resolution was not
occurring. Focusing on the depression or on the issues causing

it would have been a laborious route to relief. By focusing on stimulating, nourishing and strengthening the core belief about my value, I was able to use my energy effectively and efficiently to do what I needed to gain resolution. The root cause of the imbalance needs to be dealt with therapeutically if we find that we are in a chronic pattern.

As a rule of thumb, once we isolate the cause of a problem we will automatically begin to organize our energy to resolve the problem. However, if we focus primarily on the feeling (symptom), the feeling is intensified. By assuming that every issue/problem we encounter relates to one of the core beliefs, we change our focus from symptoms to causes.

By asking "Am I willing to believe _____?" we recognize our autonomy and stimulate our natural capacity for health. As we intentionally focus energy on our side, we begin to isolate and energize whatever belief system is not functioning at full capacity. It is unrealistic to expect ourselves to hold a perfect balance of our psychic energy in all core belief systems at all times. Intentional focusing of thought is an energy-efficient way to gain psychological balance, and something we can all do on a regular basis. Bringing our attention to a Healthy Core Belief energizes and nourishes it, but it is not a once-and-for-all process. Just as we don't assume we'll never need another drink of water after we've quenched our thirst for the moment, so activating and "feeding" Healthy Core Beliefs bring us into psychological balance for the time being, but that balance will need to be renewed and re-established over and over again.

After the first edition of this book was published, a number of people reported their difficulty and/or resistance to the question "Am I willing to believe" and suggested instead "Am I willing to acknowledge/consider/think about?" as alternatives. If one of these feel more comfortable as you do the exercises, fine, use it.

It is important however, to recognize that in confronting ourselves we are realigning our basic belief systems and resistance might be indicative of clinging to inadequate, unexamined, archaic notions. Notions that cause dissonance within or between us are always suspect. That which is ultimately true creates harmony and resonates within us. Healthy core beliefs, while on the surface simplistic and idealistic, are extremely difficult to discount. Few of us will deny, while looking at an infant, that these Healthy Core Beliefs are true. Intuitively, we also resonate to the possibilities for harmonious and creative well-being they afford humanity. I've examined them from many perspectives and have seen positive change occur as people grapple with them; I believe that, at the very least, they point us toward ultimate truth. Resistances to their truth are most likely indicators of contaminated thinking. Because "one thing leads to another and all roads lead to where you're at," easing into new beliefs will gradually lead to truth. Each person knows better than I the form of self-confrontation that will allow them to advance human esteem.

Core beliefs are to the psyche what organs are to the body. Core beliefs need constant stimulation and nourishment. A muscle loses health and tone without exercise and proper nourishment. Without stimulation and nourishment (attention and interaction), a core belief loses its vitality.

When a core belief is weak, the weakness comes to our attention as a chronic feeling (depression, frustration, anxiety, boredom, anger, etc.). Feelings are signals and can serve the same function for us psychologically as physical symptoms do physiologically. Relieving the symptom in either case may give temporary relief, but cure comes when the cause is dealt with directly. In the example of my depression, I could have turned around, gone home and spent the day in bed or gone to a movie. Either would have provided some relief for the depressive symptoms. But the depression would not have been resolved on a causal level because I would not have recognized its source. By focusing on the core belief, I found the *cause* and began to resolve the issues underlying the depression.

While the process seems simple, the application of the process requires sensitivity to our internal workings. We're complex and changing organisms and our attention to our own processes needs to be constant, *gentle* and positive. There is no once-and-for-all meal (nourishment) or exercise (stimulation) for the physical body and there is no once-and-for-all way to support our core beliefs. Physical conditioning allows us to deal with physical issues. Intentional core belief strengthening allows us to deal with psychological and sociological issues.

Thoughts, Feelings and Actions

Thoughts are both spontaneous and intentional. Once a thought/idea is formulated, a biochemical process occurs which we recognize as a feeling. As you read this, if your attention is diverted by someone screaming, within an instant your whole body will feel alarmed and you may act on the feeling. This is a spontaneous movement from thought to feeling to action.

On the other hand, if you direct your thought to a problem, a plan or a pleasant memory, within seconds your whole system will begin to feel the experiences associated with that thought, and ultimately the feeling will seek resolution through action. A good example of this is an erotic fantasy.

Whenever we have an erotic fantasy we quickly experience the physiological excitement associated with sex. Imagine that you are enjoying an erotic fantasy and through the window you notice your child run into the busy street. Your feelings quickly change from pleasure to alarm. A rule of thumb is "where the head is, the body goes." Each of these thoughts create a feeling.

Feelings, I want to emphasize, are indications of a need for action. Feelings left unattended become more and more pronounced until they dominate our attention. This is a healthy function. The more rapidly I attend to a feeling, the more fluid my life experience, the greater my sense of autonomy.

On the next page is a lighthearted illustration of what happens as we travel on the "Life Plane" with and without adequate foundational core beliefs.

Whenever the "now" issue is experienced as a problem, that problem is brought to our attention by a recurring feeling that can cause us to lose our momentum and balance, just like the fellow on the next page. This loss of equilibrium is how our system indicates that a core belief is not strong enough at the moment for us to successfully resolve an issue at hand.

By raising the question "Am I willing to believe that I am _____?" we begin to strengthen core beliefs by focusing our thoughts. If we experience an internal resistance to affirm any core belief, we begin to wonder "Why am I unwilling to believe I am _____?" When we experience internal affirmation of our capability, power, lovability, value and equality, we begin to deal with "what *is* right now" and get on with our life.

It is important to remember that the length of time it takes to bring an issue to resolution is not as important as the fact that *it is moving*, however slowly, toward resolution. It takes about 20 years for a child to mature, and as long as one stage follows another step-by-step, the child is growing toward maturity and the process can be enjoyed by both parent and child. It is primarily when we are stuck on an issue, and it doesn't seem to be moving toward resolution, that life becomes overwhelming.

Life Energy

Energy runs either creatively or defensively. The following figure illustrates life energy:

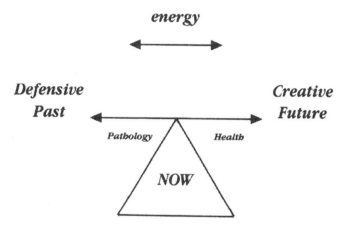

A simple but profound way of understanding life is to see it as an exchange of energy. This energy exchange is easily observed in ourselves—stimulus created by an outside event or internal awareness develops into a thought and results in a feeling which can be transformed into an action. As an example of how this works, you might try recalling an incident when someone stood by you in a difficult time. As you think about this, notice what you are feeling. Most likely you will have a natural desire to act on the feeling—either by calling or writing to the person, sharing your memories with a friend, or even just acknowledging it to yourself. Feelings change regularly with our change of focus. Energy is constantly transformed; to remember that we are *always* transforming, consciously or not, will enhance our ability to *choose intentionally* how we will transform it. Transforming energy into action that enhances our life and the lives of others is indicative of using energy creatively. Transforming energy into protecting our ideas, actions or territory is indicative of defense. To the extent we see that we have a choice we will experience ourselves as self-directed, which leads to a fulfilled and purposeful life rather than one that seems empty and meaningless. A sense of personal fulfillment always attends those times when we know we are using our energy creatively to address the issues, causes, jobs and activities that are truly important to us.

Establishing Healthy Core Beliefs

When we plant a tree in our yard we prepare the ground, plant the tree and attend to it closely until it is well-rooted. After it's established we attend to it regularly to see that it stays healthy. The same process applies in the establishment and maintenance of Healthy Core Beliefs.

Preparation of the ground can be compared to a rational understanding that Healthy Core Beliefs are the basis of Human Esteem. If you have read this far and are considering the ideas that one, simple truths have far-reaching implications and two, core beliefs establish healthy Human Esteem, you have prepared the ground.

Thinking over our core beliefs about ourselves and others provides us with a way to get to the heart of issues as they arise. Although many of the concepts discussed in this book are not new, and in fact most of them probably ring true and even "sound familiar" to you, I believe that spelling them out and refining them to five basic categories provides a model to organize and utilize the truths and knowledge each of us has accumulated thus far. By paying close and systematic attention to the strength of our own beliefs about ourselves and others, we can learn to support our autonomy regardless of circumstances.

The Healthy Core Belief Workbook offers a systematic way to nourish these ideas during a five-week period. The Workbook will help exercise, nourish and strengthen the core beliefs. Some of the exercises will seem easy and some difficult; when we run into a core belief that is a "stumbling block" for us, it indicates a need for greater thought on that particular subject. Once we've thought through a new idea or experience it is possible to assimilate it without "stumbling."

Through the years I've found that behaviors change when we concentrate on taking up *new* behavior. We've been taught that behavior changes through discipline and by concentrating on giving up old behavior (bad habits), but I've never found this to be effective. This fact is best illustrated by New Year's resolutions. New Year's resolutions simply don't work well because when we concentrate on giving something up we're left in a psychological vacuum. As much as we dislike a habit, the habit does provide something for us, even if nothing more than stimulation and structure. At the very least, the stimulation and structure needs to be replaced before we can readily change behavior. As I mentioned earlier, when I quit smoking, I spent most of the time I had previously spent smoking talking about not smoking. New behavior is the hallmark of change. Change occurs first in thought. New thoughts create new feelings and new feelings encourage new actions.

The Workbook offers daily exercises that require only five to 10 minutes in the morning and five to 10 minutes in the evening. To do all the exercises will take five full weeks, with two days off each week. Too often in our zeal for personal improvement we neglect to give ourselves time off to relax and assimilate—this overworking generally tends to retard our creativity and growth.

As you do the exercises remember to *be gentle*. As you listen to the internal dialogue keep asking: "How am I treating myself? Am I on my side or on my case?"

True change is subtle—not necessarily dramatic. True change is like a seed planted, quickened and growing. True change is attended by predominantly calm and warm feelings. As you go through the Workbook, if the process is not feeling like natural growth, check to see if you are being gentle with yourself. You probably are not staying on your side.

The five healthy core beliefs are the basis of transacting from the "I'm OK, you're OK" position originally identified by Eric Berne in *Transactional Analysis In Psychotherapy* and popularized by Thomas and Amy Harris in *I'm OK, You're OK*. "I'm okay, you're okay" is a very fetching idea and one that intrigues, but for most of us, is little more than naive, aphoristic and characteristic of pop psychology. Reexamining the concept of "OKness" in light of healthy core beliefs undergirds the idea with a substantive theory. Once the implicit beliefs behind Berne's intuition that "I'm OK, you're OK" are exposed this "fetching" idea can become a solid base for fulfilling interaction. We all yearn to experience ourselves as okay and our lives as meaningful and purposeful. Meaning and purpose will elude us when we are unable to maintain our sense of OKness. This book attempts to make evident the foundation of OKness in an effort to demonstrate the necessity of human esteem. "I'm OK, you're OK" is an idea that points to a truth beyond itself; I believe Human Esteem serves the same purpose.

Without Healthy Core Beliefs, adequately nourished and fully functioning, our sense of OKness will be transient at best. We have little or no control over much of what we must deal with every day from economic conditions, social change, behavior of our friends and families, to traffic conditions. On the whole, we cannot control much of what we encounter in our lives, though in many instances we are not without influence. Until we recognize that our primary source of control is in taking charge of ourselves, we will experience ourselves as not OK and are likely to fail to influence situations effectively. Most of us have been led to believe that when things are going badly, it means we are at fault. Perceiving ourselves at fault in situations that we have no control over places us at the mercy of circumstances and subverts the power we have to influence change. Once we change our thinking and recognize that we are capable, powerful, valuable, lovable and equal, we're free to look for ways to resolve the inequities we experience. Just as a house will withstand a storm to the extent that it is well-built and has an adequate foundation, so a person will withstand the vicissitudes of life when healthy core beliefs are well-nourished and functioning.

As we recognize that our basic equilibrium is in our charge, we will engage the day-to-day realities appropriately. The Workbook is designed to initiate the shift from self-image being controlled by other people and times to the true self emerging from within.

It is always advantageous to develop support systems when we are realigning our beliefs and this support greatly heightens the development of autonomy and Human Esteem. You'll know you have established adequate Healthy Core beliefs when you are increasingly aware that all people are capable, powerful, valuable, lovable and equal. This recognition is the hallmark of Human Esteem.

The Implications of
Healthy Esteem

Ideally children should not grow up without the knowledge that they are capable, powerful, valuable, lovable and equal. And ideally adults do not have to live without this knowledge, even if they were not taught it as children. Adults are responsible for stimulating, nourishing and strengthening their own core beliefs, maintaining Human Esteem and developing their autonomy.

Once these core beliefs are strong in us and we recognize these same qualities in all people, we will feel as if we have had a revelation which will begin a revolution—an "about-face" in our thought and action. This is why I said in the beginning that simple truths are like time bombs. I've never been the same since I first read Eric Berne's words that every child is born a prince or princess. Berne's simple statement was a revelation to me about myself and it started a revolution in my thought. I now know that I am a capable, powerful, valuable, lovable and equal human. *Revelation precedes revolution.* Thinking of ourselves and others from an attitude of Human Esteem can cause a personal revelation that brings us to reexamine cultural values. George Leonard recognized this in his book *The Silent Pulse* when he said "Obviously the time is past for us to consider the self as doggedly separate from and opposed to the rest of existence. This tragic dichotomy, between self and other, along with the glorification of competition and winning, and general selfishness, might have worked in the days of the frontier but in recent years it has led unerringly to Vietnam and Watergate and the energy, ecology, and economic crises. Simple historical logic...urges that we transform our values and behavior." With a revolution of Human Esteem we all stand to win as we create processes that solve human problems equitably, from personal to international.

Human Esteem Workbook

The Beginning...
If I don't take what I read
or what I am told and weigh it against
my own experience, then of what
value am I to myself?

Hugh Prather

All the good ideas and inspirational thoughts in the world do us little or no good until we systematically apply them to our own experience. The Workbook section is the "proof of the pudding" of Healthy Core Beliefs. We suggest that you use the Workbook pages as well as a personal journal as the first step to integrating these ideas into your own internal support system.

Take the difficulties in your life and use them in conjunction with the workbook to more powerfully integrate the Healthy Core Beliefs into your life: Be aware of the option to feel capable, powerful, valuable, lovable and equal in moments of stress. *The truth is in the body.* As you repeat the thought for the day, you will experience subtle sensations which, when you focus on them, will have a message for you. Discuss your reactions in the Workbook and in your own journal.

If you choose to use the Workbook, do the process at your own pace, for yourself, and not in compliance or adaptation to an outside force (including the authors of this book!).

DAY 1

Capable means I have the skills necessary to pursue my wants and realize many of my ambitions.

IN THE MORNING

Ask yourself this question a minimum of ten times:

Am I willing to believe that I am capable?

- Now pay attention to what you're experiencing in your body.
- Be aware of any sensations or feelings.
- What are these feelings telling you?
- Ask yourself what the message of the sensation is and make a note of your answer.

SENSATION   MESSAGE

_____   _____

_____   _____

_____   _____

_____   _____

THROUGHOUT THE DAY

Each time you feel tension, recall the question:

Am I willing to believe that I am a capable human being?

BEDTIME

As you go to bed, meditate on the statement for the day at the top of this page. Write any thoughts in your journal.

❧ Be Gentle ❧

DAY 2

> *Capable means I have the ability to contribute to the well-being of myself and others.*

IN THE MORNING

Ask yourself this question a minimum of ten times:
Am I willing to believe that I am capable?

- Now pay attention to what you're experiencing in your body.
- Be aware of any sensations or feelings.
- What are these feelings telling you?
- Ask yourself what the message of the sensation is and make a note of your answer.

SENSATION	MESSAGE
_____	_____
_____	_____
_____	_____
_____	_____

THROUGHOUT THE DAY

Each time you feel tension, recall the question:
Am I willing to believe that I am a capable human being?

BEDTIME

As you go to bed, meditate on the statement for the day at the top of this page. Write any thoughts in your journal.

❧ Be Gentle ❧

DAY 3

> *Capable means I have the ability to cope with what*
> *life is, right here now, however difficult.*

IN THE MORNING

Ask yourself this question a minimum of ten times:

Am I willing to believe that I am capable?

- Now pay attention to what you're experiencing in your body.
- Be aware of any sensations or feelings.
- What are these feelings telling you?
- Ask yourself what the message of the sensation is and make a note of your answer.

SENSATION	MESSAGE
_____	_____
_____	_____
_____	_____
_____	_____

THROUGHOUT THE DAY

Each time you feel tension, recall the question:

Am I willing to believe that I am a capable human being?

BEDTIME

As you go to bed, meditate on the statement for the day at the top of this page. Write any thoughts in your journal.

❧ *Be Gentle* ❧

DAY 4

> *Capable means I have the ability to develop and sustain*
> *nourishing and stimulating contact with others.*

IN THE MORNING

Ask yourself this question a minimum of ten times:

Am I willing to believe that I am capable?

- Now pay attention to what you're experiencing in your body.
- Be aware of any sensations or feelings.
- What are these feelings telling you?
- Ask yourself what the message of the sensation is and make a note of your answer.

SENSATION   MESSAGE

_____   _____

_____   _____

_____   _____

_____   _____

THROUGHOUT THE DAY

Each time you feel tension, recall the question:

Am I willing to believe that I am a capable human being?

BEDTIME

As you go to bed, meditate on the statement for the day at
the top of this page. Write any thoughts in your journal.

⊰ *Be Gentle* ⊱

DAY 5

Capable means that I and others can peacefully resolve problems.

IN THE MORNING

Ask yourself this question a minimum of ten times:

Am I willing to believe that I am capable?

- Now pay attention to what you're experiencing in your body.
- Be aware of any sensations or feelings.
- What are these feelings telling you?
- Ask yourself what the message of the sensation is and make a note of your answer.

SENSATION	MESSAGE
_____	_____
_____	_____
_____	_____
_____	_____

THROUGHOUT THE DAY

Each time you feel tension, recall the question:

Am I willing to believe that I am a capable human being?

BEDTIME

As you go to bed, meditate on the statement for the day at the top of this page. Write any thoughts in your journal.

❧ Be Gentle ❧

DAY 1

> *Powerful means that I recognize and acknowledge*
> *my influence and choose how I will use it.*

IN THE MORNING

Ask yourself this question a minimum of ten times:

Am I willing to believe that I am powerful?

- Now pay attention to what you're experiencing in your body.
- Be aware of any sensations or feelings.
- What are these feelings telling you?
- Ask yourself what the message of the sensation is and make a note of your answer.

SENSATION	MESSAGE
_____	_____
_____	_____
_____	_____
_____	_____

THROUGHOUT THE DAY

Each time you feel tension, recall the question:

Am I willing to believe that I am a powerful human being?

BEDTIME

As you go to bed, meditate on the statement for the day at the top of this page. Write any thoughts in your journal.

⊰ Be Gentle ⊱

DAY 2_____

> *Powerful means that every bite of food I eat*
> *becomes energy I utilize to express myself in the*
> *world.*

IN THE MORNING

Ask yourself this question a minimum of ten times:

Am I willing to believe that I am powerful?

- Now pay attention to what you're experiencing in your body.
- Be aware of any sensations or feelings.
- What are these feelings telling you?
- Ask yourself what the message of the sensation is and make a note of your answer.

      SENSATION   MESSAGE

_____ _____

_____ _____

_____ _____

_____ _____

THROUGHOUT THE DAY

Each time you feel tension, recall the question:

Am I willing to believe that I am a powerful human being?

BEDTIME

As you go to bed, meditate on the statement for the day at the top of this page. Write any thoughts in your journal.

❧ Be Gentle ❧

DAY 3_____

> *Powerful means that others respond to me by the*
> *way I present myself.*

IN THE MORNING

Ask yourself this question a minimum of ten times:

Am I willing to believe that I am powerful?

- Now pay attention to what you're experiencing in your body.
- Be aware of any sensations or feelings.
- What are these feelings telling you?
- Ask yourself what the message of the sensation is and make a note of your answer.

SENSATION	MESSAGE
_____	_____
_____	_____
_____	_____
_____	_____

THROUGHOUT THE DAY

Each time you feel tension, recall the question:

Am I willing to believe that I am a powerful human being?

BEDTIME

As you go to bed, meditate on the statement for the day at the top of this page. Write any thoughts in your journal.

❧ Be Gentle ❧

DAY 4 _____

> *Powerful means that I shape today along with the*
> *five billion others who share this period of history.*

IN THE MORNING

Ask yourself this question a minimum of ten times:

Am I willing to believe that I am powerful?

- Now pay attention to what you're experiencing in your body.
- Be aware of any sensations or feelings.
- What are these feelings telling you?
- Ask yourself what the message of the sensation is and make a note of your answer.

SENSATION	MESSAGE
_____	_____
_____	_____
_____	_____
_____	_____

THROUGHOUT THE DAY

Each time you feel tension, recall the question:

Am I willing to believe that I am a powerful human being?

BEDTIME

As you go to bed, meditate on the statement for the day at the top of this page. Write any thoughts in your journal.

❧ Be Gentle ❧

DAY 5

> *Powerful means that I have as much influence on those around me as they have on me.*

IN THE MORNING

Ask yourself this question a minimum of ten times:

Am I willing to believe that I am powerful?

- Now pay attention to what you're experiencing in your body.
- Be aware of any sensations or feelings.
- What are these feelings telling you?
- Ask yourself what the message of the sensation is and make a note of your answer.

SENSATION   MESSAGE

_____   _____

_____   _____

_____   _____

_____   _____

THROUGHOUT THE DAY

Each time you feel tension, recall the question:

Am I willing to believe that I am a powerful human being?

BEDTIME

As you go to bed, meditate on the statement for the day at the top of this page. Write any thoughts in your journal.

◈ Be Gentle ◈

DAY 1 _____

> *Valuable means that I have worth because I exist.*

IN THE MORNING

Ask yourself this question a minimum of ten times:

Am I willing to believe that I am valuable?

- Now pay attention to what you're experiencing in your body.
- Be aware of any sensations or feelings.
- What are these feelings telling you?
- Ask yourself what the message of the sensation is and make a note of your answer.

SENSATION	MESSAGE
_____	_____
_____	_____
_____	_____
_____	_____

THROUGHOUT THE DAY

Each time you feel tension, recall the question:

Am I willing to believe that I am a valuable human being?

BEDTIME

As you go to bed, meditate on the statement for the day at the top of this page. Write any thoughts in your journal.

❧ Be Gentle ❧

DAY 2

Valuable means I have something to offer.

IN THE MORNING

Ask yourself this question a minimum of ten times:

Am I willing to believe that I am valuable?

- Now pay attention to what you're experiencing in your body.
- Be aware of any sensations or feelings.
- What are these feelings telling you?
- Ask yourself what the message of the sensation is and make a note of your answer.

SENSATION   MESSAGE

_____   _____

_____   _____

_____   _____

_____   _____

THROUGHOUT THE DAY

Each time you feel tension, recall the question:

Am I willing to believe that I am a valuable human being?

BEDTIME

As you go to bed, meditate on the statement for the day at the top of this page. Write any thoughts in your journal.

❦ Be Gentle ❧

DAY 3_____

Valuable means that I can enjoy myself and others.

IN THE MORNING

Ask yourself this question a minimum of ten times:

Am I willing to believe that I am valuable?

- Now pay attention to what you're experiencing in your body.
- Be aware of any sensations or feelings.
- What are these feelings telling you?
- Ask yourself what the message of the sensation is and make a note of your answer.

SENSATION   MESSAGE

_____   _____

_____   _____

_____   _____

_____   _____

THROUGHOUT THE DAY

Each time you feel tension, recall the question:

Am I willing to believe that I am a valuable human being?

BEDTIME

As you go to bed, meditate on the statement for the day at
the top of this page. Write any thoughts in your journal.

❧ Be Gentle ❧

DAY 4

> *Valuable means I accept my importance.*

IN THE MORNING

Ask yourself this question a minimum of ten times:

Am I willing to believe that I am valuable?

- Now pay attention to what you're experiencing in your body.
- Be aware of any sensations or feelings.
- What are these feelings telling you?
- Ask yourself what the message of the sensation is and make a note of your answer.

SENSATION   MESSAGE

_____   _____

_____   _____

_____   _____

_____   _____

THROUGHOUT THE DAY

Each time you feel tension, recall the question:

Am I willing to believe that I am a valuable human being?

BEDTIME

As you go to bed, meditate on the statement for the day at the top of this page. Write any thoughts in your journal.

❧ Be Gentle ❧

DAY 5

> *Valuable means there is sense to every aspect of my experience.*

IN THE MORNING

Ask yourself this question a minimum of ten times:
Am I willing to believe that I am valuable?

- Now pay attention to what you're experiencing in your body.
- Be aware of any sensations or feelings.
- What are these feelings telling you?
- Ask yourself what the message of the sensation is and make a note of your answer.

SENSATION	MESSAGE
_____	_____
_____	_____
_____	_____
_____	_____

THROUGHOUT THE DAY

Each time you feel tension, recall the question:
Am I willing to believe that I am a valuable human being?

BEDTIME

As you go to bed, meditate on the statement for the day at the top of this page. Write any thoughts in your journal.

❧ Be Gentle ❧

DAY 1

> *Lovable means I can relate to myself and others in*
> *a warm and nourishing way.*

IN THE MORNING

Ask yourself this question a minimum of ten times:

Am I willing to believe that I am lovable?

- Now pay attention to what you're experiencing in your body.
- Be aware of any sensations or feelings.
- What are these feelings telling you?
- Ask yourself what the message of the sensation is and make a note of your answer.

SENSATION	MESSAGE
_____	_____
_____	_____
_____	_____
_____	_____

THROUGHOUT THE DAY

Each time you feel tension, recall the question:

Am I willing to believe that I am a lovable human being?

BEDTIME

As you go to bed, meditate on the statement for the day at the top of this page. Write any thoughts in your journal.

❧ Be Gentle ❧

DAY 2_____

> *Lovable means that each feeling I have is unique.*

IN THE MORNING

Ask yourself this question a minimum of ten times:

Am I willing to believe that I am lovable?

- Now pay attention to what you're experiencing in your body.
- Be aware of any sensations or feelings.
- What are these feelings telling you?
- Ask yourself what the message of the sensation is and make a note of your answer.

SENSATION	MESSAGE
_____	_____
_____	_____
_____	_____
_____	_____

THROUGHOUT THE DAY

Each time you feel tension, recall the question:

Am I willing to believe that I am a lovable human being?

BEDTIME

As you go to bed, meditate on the statement for the day at the top of this page. Write any thoughts in your journal.

❧ Be Gentle ❧

DAY 3

Lovable means that I feel I am an individual and precious to myself and others.

IN THE MORNING

Ask yourself this question a minimum of ten times:

Am I willing to believe that I am lovable?

- Now pay attention to what you're experiencing in your body.
- Be aware of any sensations or feelings.
- What are these feelings telling you?
- Ask yourself what the message of the sensation is and make a note of your answer.

SENSATION   MESSAGE

_____   _____

_____   _____

_____   _____

_____

THROUGHOUT THE DAY

Each time you feel tension, recall the question:

Am I willing to believe that I am a lovable human being?

BEDTIME

As you go to bed, meditate on the statement for the day at the top of this page. Write any thoughts in your journal.

Be Gentle

DAY 4

> *Lovable means that I grow and have a sense of well-being when I give and receive nurturing.*

IN THE MORNING

Ask yourself this question a minimum of ten times:

Am I willing to believe that I am lovable?

- Now pay attention to what you're experiencing in your body.
- Be aware of any sensations or feelings.
- What are these feelings telling you?
- Ask yourself what the message of the sensation is and make a note of your answer.

SENSATION	MESSAGE
_____	_____
_____	_____
_____	_____
_____	_____

THROUGHOUT THE DAY

Each time you feel tension, recall the question:

Am I willing to believe that I am a lovable human being?

BEDTIME

As you go to bed, meditate on the statement for the day at the top of this page. Write any thoughts in your journal.

❧ Be Gentle ❧

DAY 4

> *Lovable means that I can create environments in which the human spirit will flourish.*

IN THE MORNING

Ask yourself this question a minimum of ten times:

Am I willing to believe that I am lovable?

- Now pay attention to what you're experiencing in your body.
- Be aware of any sensations or feelings.
- What are these feelings telling you?
- Ask yourself what the message of the sensation is and make a note of your answer.

SENSATION   MESSAGE

_____   _____

_____   _____

_____   _____

_____   _____

THROUGHOUT THE DAY

Each time you feel tension, recall the question:

Am I willing to believe that I am a lovable human being?

BEDTIME

As you go to bed, meditate on the statement for the day at the top of this page. Write any thoughts in your journal.

❧ *Be Gentle* ❧

DAY 1 _____

> *Equal means that I am not better than or worse than anyone else.*

IN THE MORNING

Ask yourself this question a minimum of ten times:

Am I willing to believe that I am equal?

- Now pay attention to what you're experiencing in your body.
- Be aware of any sensations or feelings.
- What are these feelings telling you?
- Ask yourself what the message of the sensation is and make a note of your answer.

SENSATION   MESSAGE

_____   _____

_____   _____

_____   _____

_____   _____

THROUGHOUT THE DAY

Each time you feel tension, recall the question:

Am I willing to believe that I am an equal human being?

BEDTIME

As you go to bed, meditate on the statement for the day at the top of this page. Write any thoughts in your journal.

❧ Be Gentle ❧

DAY 2

Equal means we are all part of the whole.

IN THE MORNING

Ask yourself this question a minimum of ten times:
Am I willing to believe that I am equal?

- Now pay attention to what you're experiencing in your body.
- Be aware of any sensations or feelings.
- What are these feelings telling you?
- Ask yourself what the message of the sensation is and make a note of your answer.

SENSATION   MESSAGE

_____   _____

_____   _____

_____   _____

_____   _____

THROUGHOUT THE DAY

Each time you feel tension, recall the question:
Am I willing to believe that I am an equal human being?

BEDTIME

As you go to bed, meditate on the statement for the day at
the top of this page. Write any thoughts in your journal.

❧ Be Gentle ❧

DAY 3

> *Equal means that the person next to me is just as challenged by life as I am.*

IN THE MORNING

Ask yourself this question a minimum of ten times:
Am I willing to believe that I am equal?

- Now pay attention to what you're experiencing in your body.
- Be aware of any sensations or feelings.
- What are these feelings telling you?
- Ask yourself what the message of the sensation is and make a note of your answer.

SENSATION   MESSAGE

_____   _____

_____   _____

_____   _____

_____   _____

THROUGHOUT THE DAY

Each time you feel tension, recall the question:
Am I willing to believe that I am an equal human being?

BEDTIME

As you go to bed, meditate on the statement for the day at the top of this page. Write any thoughts in your journal.

❧ Be Gentle ❧

DAY 4

> *Equal means my problems are*
> *no larger than my abilities.*

IN THE MORNING

Ask yourself this question a minimum of ten times:
Am I willing to believe that I am equal?

- Now pay attention to what you're experiencing in your body.
- Be aware of any sensations or feelings.
- What are these feelings telling you?
- Ask yourself what the message of the sensation is and make a note of your answer.

SENSATION   MESSAGE

_____   _____

_____   _____

_____   _____

_____   _____

THROUGHOUT THE DAY

Each time you feel tension, recall the question:
Am I willing to believe that I am an equal human being?

BEDTIME

As you go to bed, meditate on the statement for the day at
the top of this page. Write any thoughts in your journal.

Be Gentle

DAY 5

> *Equal means that I and others can*
> *peacefully resolve problems.*

IN THE MORNING

Ask yourself this question a minimum of ten times:
Am I willing to believe that I am equal?

- Now pay attention to what you're experiencing in your body.
- Be aware of any sensations or feelings.
- What are these feelings telling you?
- Ask yourself what the message of the sensation is and make a note of your answer.

SENSATION	MESSAGE
_____	_____
_____	_____
_____	_____
_____	_____

THROUGHOUT THE DAY

Each time you feel tension, recall the question:
Am I willing to believe that I am an equal human being?

BEDTIME

As you go to bed, meditate on the statement for the day at
the top of this page. Write any thoughts in your journal.

❧ Be Gentle ❧

DAY 5

> *Equal means that I and others can*
> *peacefully resolve problems.*

IN THE MORNING

Ask yourself this question a minimum of ten times:

Am I willing to believe that I am equal?

- Now pay attention to what you're experiencing in your body.
- Be aware of any sensations or feelings.
- What are these feelings telling you?
- Ask yourself what the message of the sensation is and make a note of your answer.

SENSATION	MESSAGE
_____	_____
_____	_____
_____	_____
_____	_____

THROUGHOUT THE DAY

Each time you feel tension, recall the question:

Am I willing to believe that I am an equal human being?

BEDTIME

As you go to bed, meditate on the statement for the day at the top of this page. Write any thoughts in your journal.

❦ Be Gentle ❧

From Human Esteem
to Peacemaking

When we possess a healthy sense of our autonomy, we are no longer willing to define ourselves by what we are against; instead we define and direct ourselves by what we are for.

Not too long after I began to use core belief therapy and had spent some time supporting and strengthening my own health, I began to ask the question: "What do I want to be now?" As I reviewed the options available, I discovered that our culture's symbols of success were all open to me: wealth, power, fame and pseudo-sainthood. I realized that if I wanted to pursue wealth, I could put my ideas together and organize my energy around the pursuit of money. If I wanted to pursue power, I could direct my energy, friends, organizations and time so that I could accumulate power. If I wanted to pursue fame, I could arrange people and events so that I captured the spotlight. And if I wanted to be a saint, I could pursue some worthy cause in a pseudo-humble way and get people to view me as "some kind of saint."

I saw all of these as large tasks, but within my grasp if I was willing to make one or more of them my goal. I turned each option and every possible combination of options over in my mind but didn't find anything I wanted to spend my life pursuing. I began to puzzle over the question, "what do I want to do?" as I wrestled with what some call "mid-life crisis." I describe it as the "third score." We spend the first score (20 years) of life gathering information and instructions; the second score proving that the information and instructions work or don't work; and during the "third score" we wake up to the fact that our life is *our life*. Ultimately we make our life what it is. Past instruction can be useful but it need not be the exclusive driving force.

Once I'm aware that I am capable, powerful, valuable, lovable and equal, I am free to decide what I will do. At one time I decided to be a minister and went about doing what was necessary to become one. Later I decided to become a psychotherapist, and did what was necessary to become one. I've decided on many goals, skills and adventures throughout my life, and as long as I felt I was capable, powerful, valuable, lovable and equal, I could put my energies into accomplishing those goals.

The *process* is important. First we affirm that we are adequate, next we direct our energy toward achieving our goal, and finally we create an acceptable solution. This is not to imply that we can be or do anything we want to be or do on a whim. But it is to say: as long as we're willing to believe that we're capable, powerful, valuable, lovable and equal, we can decide to be what we want and systematically pursue it to a satisfactory resolution. Sometimes a satisfactory resolution may include changing our goals.

It seemed to me that questions of being are the outcome of this process and so I began to ask myself, "What do I **want to be?**" The idea that most interested me was, "Am I willing to be a peacemaker?" I decided that for the next six months I would utilize my "rambling/rumbling" thought time to the question, "Am I willing to be a peacemaker?" This question initiated the most exciting journey thus far in my life.

What happened to me as I systematically and intentionally asked myself, "Am I willing to be a peacemaker?" was stimulating and creative. I found solutions to many of the objections I'd previously had to being a peacemaker. I'd objected to giving my life entirely to the peace efforts I was familiar with because much of the energy in peace movements is directed toward what people are against. I was aware that many peacemakers are paradoxically caught in the bind of being so against war that they will go to war to stop war. I did not want to spend the rest of my days defining myself by what I consider history's and our culture's insanity. As I asked myself, "Am I willing to be a peacemaker?" my creative energies engaged and I began to realize that I could be pro-active (defining myself by what I am *for*) rather than re-active (defining myself by what I am *against*). I could define myself by what I was for and I could teach others how to do that. Rather than going over the same things again and again (thinking more and more about less and less) I began to stimulate new thought as I confronted myself with the question, "Am I willing to be a peacemaker?" I encountered the most exciting possibilities for my life that I'd ever contemplated. This occurred because I was operating on well-nourished and well-stimulated core beliefs. I had developed a new sense of autonomy and my creative energy rose to a new level.

The question you ask may be different from mine, but when you've completed the Workbook, you will be prepared to act with a new sense of autonomy.

As I have suggested, there *is* a relationship between personal peace and world peace. Viktor Frankl recognized during his internment at Auschwitz that "Fear makes come true that which one is afraid of." The truth of the self-fulfilling prophecy can apply in both a positive and a negative sense. The state of personal peace individuals maintain will ultimately determine the state of peace in the world. Just as our personal state has far-reaching effects on the temperament of the world, so the temperament of the world has far-reaching effects on our personal state. Once we are aware of this cycle of influence we are able to see that things which appear separate are connected. As we recognize this unity, we realize that our personal peace contributes directly to the peace of the world. This awareness helps us realize that the establishment of world peace will ultimately begin in our personal lives.

Human esteem is the essential ingredient we need to experience ourselves as individuals who are autonomous, yet capable of collaborating with others in making peace. While it is easy to see how viewing another person as an opponent establishes a polarity that can propel us toward defensiveness and finally war, it is not quite as easy to see how maintaining human esteem can propel us toward peace—but the logic is the same. It is not as easy for us to see this logic in peacemaking because we have been so highly conditioned in oppositional problem-solving and our conditioning in collaborative problem-solving is limited.

When peace is in our individual lives and our relational/social systems we are willing to trust that we have the power to make peace. The five foundational core beliefs, when fully operational, cause us to recognize that we are ultimately responsible for what beliefs we hold. At the moment we decide to trust our capacities to *do, be and think*, our sense of autonomy emerges and we recognize that we can intentionally and deliberately mobilize our energy to create peace.

The day our family moved into our new home, my sons complained to my wife and I that they did not like the kids in the new neighborhood. Seeing no reason for our sons not to like the new kids, my wife asked, "Why don't you like them?" My youngest son, then four, said "We don't like them because we don't know them." His clarity helped us resolve the situation.

Autonomy is the power to govern our lives. By knowing specifically what the issue was with our children we were able to act effectively. This same power to govern our lives emerges when we are fully aware that all humans are capable, powerful, valuable, lovable and equal. As we know clearly that we have the power to resolve the dilemmas that create life-threatening stresses, we can move decisively in the direction of peace.

The Workbook will help you build the knowledge that you are capable, powerful, valuable, lovable and equal. Once we establish this knowledge in ourselves we are encouraged to decide to trust each other. With the decision to trust based on well-established core beliefs, we find ways to exercise our autonomy in effective peaceful action. When enough of us exercise our autonomy in peaceful ways, we will change from *oppositional* to *mutual* problem-solving methods. We will be aware of our autonomy and free to collaborate in peacemaking.

DAY 1

> *Peacemaking is a "here and now" experience that I*
> *can participate in during ordinary, daily events.*

IN THE MORNING

Ask yourself this question a minimum of ten times:

Am I willing to believe that I am a peacemaker?

- Now pay attention to what you're experiencing in your body.
- Be aware of any sensations or feelings.
- What are these feelings telling you?
- Ask yourself what the message of the sensation is and make a note of your answer.

SENSATION   MESSAGE

_____   _____

_____   _____

_____   _____

_____   _____

THROUGHOUT THE DAY

Each time you feel tension, recall the question:

Am I willing to believe that I am a peaceful human being?

BEDTIME

As you go to bed, meditate on the statement for the day at the top of this page. Write any thoughts in your journal.

✃ *Be Gentle* ❧

DAY 2

Peacemaking is being gently and firmly for what I want life to be.

IN THE MORNING

Ask yourself this question a minimum of ten times:

Am I willing to believe that I am a peacemaker?

- Now pay attention to what you're experiencing in your body.
- Be aware of any sensations or feelings.
- What are these feelings telling you?
- Ask yourself what the message of the sensation is and make a note of your answer.

SENSATION	MESSAGE
_____	_____
_____	_____
_____	_____
_____	_____

THROUGHOUT THE DAY

Each time you feel tension, recall the question:

Am I willing to believe that I am a peaceful human being?

BEDTIME

As you go to bed, meditate on the statement for the day at the top of this page. Write any thoughts in your journal.

❧ Be Gentle ❧

DAY 3

> *Peacemaking is knowing we all create our history*
> *together—for good or for ill.*

IN THE MORNING

Ask yourself this question a minimum of ten times:

Am I willing to believe that I am a peacemaker?

- Now pay attention to what you're experiencing in your body.
- Be aware of any sensations or feelings.
- What are these feelings telling you?
- Ask yourself what the message of the sensation is and make a note of your answer.

SENSATION   MESSAGE

_____   _____

_____   _____

_____   _____

_____   _____

THROUGHOUT THE DAY

Each time you feel tension, recall the question:

Am I willing to believe that I am a peaceful human being?

BEDTIME

As you go to bed, meditate on the statement for the day at the top of this page. Write any thoughts in your journal.

❧ Be Gentle ❧

DAY 4

*Peacemaking is a lively and intriguing experiment
that enhances and nourishes human esteem.*

IN THE MORNING

Ask yourself this question a minimum of ten times:
Am I willing to believe that I am a peacemaker?

- Now pay attention to what you're experiencing in your body.
- Be aware of any sensations or feelings.
- What are these feelings telling you?
- Ask yourself what the message of the sensation is and make a note of your answer.

SENSATION	MESSAGE
_____	_____
_____	_____
_____	_____
_____	_____

THROUGHOUT THE DAY

Each time you feel tension, recall the question:
Am I willing to believe that I am a peaceful human being?

BEDTIME

As you go to bed, meditate on the statement for the day at
the top of this page. Write any thoughts in your journal.

Be Gentle

DAY 5

Peacemaking is loving loving / being being creating creating.

IN THE MORNING

Ask yourself this question a minimum of ten times:

Am I willing to believe that I am a peacemaker?

- Now pay attention to what you're experiencing in your body.
- Be aware of any sensations or feelings.
- What are these feelings telling you?
- Ask yourself what the message of the sensation is and make a note of your answer.

SENSATION   MESSAGE

_____   _____

_____   _____

_____   _____

_____   _____

THROUGHOUT THE DAY

Each time you feel tension, recall the question:

Am I willing to believe that I am a peaceful human being?

BEDTIME

As you go to bed, meditate on the statement for the day at the top of this page. Write any thoughts in your journal.

❧ Be Gentle ❧

PEACE IS...

> *Peace is around us, above us, within us.*
> *When we meet the peacemakers, they will be us.*

ON EACH DAY OF THE WEEK, WRITE IN YOUR JOURNAL
ON THE FOLLOWING STATEMENTS:

DAY 1: I have always thought about peace in the following terms:

_____

_____

DAY 2: When I think about peace, what seems the most lively, inviting and inspiring about it is:

_____

_____

DAY 3: When I imagine peace in the future, I visualize:

_____

_____

DAY 4: The peace-filled experiences I remember best are:

_____

_____

DAY 5: The hallmarks of the world peace I dream of are:

_____

_____

PEACEMAKERS... _____

> *Peacemakers direct their lives*
> *even when they face many obstacles.*

ON EACH DAY OF THE WEEK, WRITE IN YOUR JOURNAL
ON THE FOLLOWING STATEMENTS:

DAY 1: Peacemaking is the science of perceiving that things that appear to be apart are one.

_____

_____

DAY 2: Peacemaking is the art of restoring love to a relationship from which it has been driven by fear and hatred.

_____

_____

DAY 3: "Public peacemaking is what we do; private peacemaking is what we are, the two are interpenetrating."

_____

_____

DAY 4: I am best at peacemaking when I...

_____

_____

DAY 5: The day before I die, I would like to be able to say "I have contributed _____ to peacemaking."

_____

_____

We hope you have enjoyed and benefited from this book.

For more resources and information please
visit **http://www.able-and-equal.me**

Take the *Able & Equal* online course.
Weekly or even daily email prompts
to work through the practices.
Optional coaching

Download Worksheets
Access the **Structural Symbiotic Systems** Paper
from the Second Edition

Learn more about Denton Roberts and the principles that
underlie the theory and practice in this book.

Connect with others who are cultivating Human Esteem
and on the Gentle Path to Peace.

For other related projects
visit **http://www.notsocommon.pub**

27045929R00111

Printed in Great Britain
by Amazon